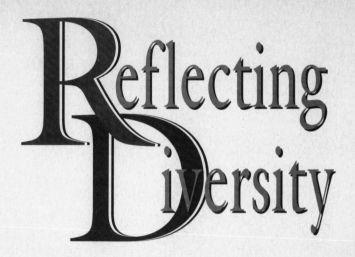

Reflecting Diversity

❖ MULTICULTURAL GUIDELINES FOR ❖
EDUCATIONAL PUBLISHING PROFESSIONALS

*"The most universal
quality is diversity."*

—*Montaigne*

MACMILLAN/McGRAW-HILL

New York ❖ Chicago ❖ Columbus

Acknowledgments

THIS GUIDE WAS PREPARED BY THE FOLLOWING MEMBERS OF THE MACMILLAN/McGRAW-HILL SCHOOL DIVISION STAFF:

Karen Baicker	Alice Dickstein	Gene McCormick
Renee Beach	Virginia Dooley	Gina Phelan
Dorrie Berkowitz	Marla Felkins	Beverly Silver
Susan Canizares	Joellyn Goodman	Susanne Singleton
Lolita Chandler	Barry Haines	Margaruite Smith
Cynthia Chapman	Marcia Hill	Anne Stribling
Thomas Condon	Lynne Jordan	Beth Beauvais Walberg
Paula Darmofal	Stacey Klaman	Felicia Wiggins
Pamela Stills Dent	Constance Keremes	Lynn Yokoe

Joyce Buckner, Director of Elementary Education,
Omaha Public School System
and member of the
reading/language arts multicultural consultant team
reviewed these guidelines.

Macmillan/McGraw-Hill School Division
10 Union Square East
New York, New York 10003

Printed in the United States of America.
ISBN 0-02-243798-3

Dedication

THIS GUIDE IS DEDICATED TO THE FOLLOWING MACMILLAN/McGRAW-HILL PROGRAM AUTHORS AND MULTICULTURAL CONSULTANTS. THEIR INSIGHTS HAVE HELPED TO INCREASE OUR AWARENESS, AND THEIR VISION HAS HELPED TO SHAPE THE PROGRAMS WE PUBLISH.

María Acosta
Rim An
Marcia Ascher
Mary Atwater
Elsie Babcock
James Banks
H. Prentice Baptiste
Yvonne Beamer
Barry Beyer
Joyce Buckner
Joann Canales
Vicki Chan
Bernard L. Charles
Elba Maldonado-Colón
Gloria Contreras
Jean Craven
Margaret C. DuGard
Kathy Escamilla
Alma Flor Ada
Alejandro Gallard
Mario Garcia

Eugene Gilliom
Helen Gillotte
Jerilyn Grignon
María Emilia Torres-
  Guzmán
Earlene Hall
Cheryl Hudson
Paul B. Janeczko
Martin Johnson
JaFran Jones
Ana Huerta-Macias
Narcita Medina
Barbara Merino
Merry M. Merryfield
Carol Mitchell
Lorraine Monroe
Oscar Muñoz
James R. Murphy
Valerie Ooka Pang
Sylvia Peña
Ivy Rawlins

Yolanda Rodriguez
Joseph B. Rubin
Rosalía Salinas
Marta Sanchez
Ramón Santiago
Ramonita Adorno de
  Santiago
Joanna Fountain-
  Schroeder
Ed Schupman
Olga Valcourt-Schwartz
Walter Secada
Mary Shamrock
Kathy Parker Sorensen
Josefina Villamil Tinajero
Clifford E. Trafzer
Hai Tran
Judith Cook Tucker
René Boyer-White
Esther Lee Yao
Claudia Zaslavsky

Photo Credits

Contents

Introduction

The purpose of *Reflecting Diversity: Multicultural Guidelines for Educational Publishing Professionals* is to provide information about the procedures and processes that Macmillan/McGraw-Hill authors, editors, and illustrators employ as they develop educational materials for students in our pluralistic society. Because our educational materials reach millions of children at a time when their views of themselves and society is taking shape, we at Macmillan/McGraw-Hill are committed to publishing materials that give children an unbiased view of the full range of human potential.

Great strides have been made toward acknowledging diversity and the full range of human potential in the last several years. No longer do textbooks depict only boys excelling in mathematics and science while girls watch from the sidelines. Asian-American, African-American, Mexican-American, and Native-American boys and girls, for example, are depicted as central characters and active problem-solvers in reading selections, thereby enabling children from diverse cultures to see themselves reflected positively in a variety of situations. The physically disabled are presented realistically and as an integral part of the human family, and the elderly are depicted as active contributors to our society. Every effort has been made to encourage a variety of viewpoints and perspectives.

Why has this happened? It has happened because countless people have spoken out against social prejudice. And in response, we have implemented the procedures and processes described in this document so as to monitor ourselves and the people who work with us as we guard against social bias and ethnocentrism. We have done this in an effort to acknowledge with respect the widely varied backgrounds and traditions of our young readers, while at the same time recognizing the common human concerns, needs, and feelings that transcend these differences.

As the next century approaches, our society grows more and more diverse as our world grows ever smaller. The children we are educating will need to be prepared for both—their own diverse society and people elsewhere whose culture it will be important for them to understand. The educational materials that we develop for children must necessarily equip them for this future.

Obviously, *Reflecting Diversity: Multicultural Guidelines for Educational Publishing Professionals* does not attempt to cover every possible situation that may arise concerning issues of diversity and multiculturalism. The document does not include a section on European Americans. Instead, it focuses on groups that have been historically omitted from educational materials. By focusing on these groups, we in no way mean to imply that European Americans are not a part of the diversity that exists in the United States. Nor do we in any way believe that the guideposts in this document can be a substitute for common sense and human understanding. Because social attitudes are constantly changing, the procedures and processes outlined here remain open to continuing refinement and reevaluation. This document does, however, accurately reflect our current publishing philosophy and does address the issues of diversity that impact on our materials.

Part I

A DEMOGRAPHIC LOOK
AT TOMORROW
by Harold Hodgkinson, Ph.D.

MULTICULTURAL EDUCATION:
FOR FREEDOM'S SAKE
by James A. Banks

A Demographic Look at Tomorrow
by Harold C. Hodgkinson, Ph.D.

Because the accuracy of demographic projections is generally very high, data from the 1990 census can be used with great confidence to predict demographic changes that are likely to occur from 1990 to 2010. These demographic changes will have major implications for education in the United States in the decades to come. Student populations are changing, and the educational community must be able to meet their changing needs.

What Did the 1990 Census Show Us?

The 1990 census figures showed us that the nation grew by 22.1 million, reaching a 1990 total of 248.7 million. Different groups grew at vastly different rates, as illustrated in the following chart:

	Growth 1980-1990 (%)	Number (M)	Percent of Total
United States	+ 9.8	248.70	100.0
European American	+ 6.0	187.20	75.2
African American	+ 13.2	29.20	12.1
Native American	+ 37.9	1.95	0.8
Asian American	+ 107.8	7.27	2.9
Hispanic American	+ 53.6	22.35	9.0

Just as different groups within the United States grew at different rates, different regions of the country did so as well. The 1990 census figures indicated that 90 percent of our growth took place in the South and West. Three states accounted for half of the nation's growth— California, Texas, and Florida. As a result, California, Texas, and Florida picked up fourteen seats in the U.S. House of Representatives, seats that were given up by Michigan, Ohio, Illinois (two seats each), and New York, which lost three.

Growth in the United States was bicoastal, with Georgia, the Carolinas, and Virginia also making large gains. The heartland and mid-Atlantic states lost population. By the time of the next U.S. census, Texas will be the second most populous state, while New York will drop to third. This decline will cost New York over one billion dollars in federal funds—funds that are distributed to states based on population rank.

It is anticipated that growth rates will continue at their uneven pace through the next decade as well, with growth concentrations in the Southeast and West. According to the Congressional Research Service, by the year 2000, California will have 50 seats in the House of Representatives, Texas will have 34 seats, and Florida will have 28 seats—for a total of 112 seats in the three states. Consequently, if these states decided to vote as a block, they would command enough votes to defeat legislation introduced by any of the other states. In addition to voting power, state rankings by population determine the amount of federal block-grant funding states will receive. These demographic factors then influence educational legislation and funding in significant ways.

The states that are growing most rapidly tend to be the states with a high percentage of culturally diverse populations, especially young culturally diverse populations. If we assume that these children will go on to graduate from high school, we can predict that the following states will have significant numbers of culturally diverse high school graduates:

District of Columbia	97.6%
Hawaii	79.7
Arizona	52.6
California	52.1
Texas	48.6
Louisiana	44.0
South Carolina	40.8
Florida	37.8

According to the 1990 census, the U.S. family made some striking changes during the decade. The "Norman Rockwell" family—a working father, housewife mother, and two children of public-school age—was indicative of only 6 percent of our nation's households in 1990. The changes in household type are illustrated in the following table:

Household	1990 Census	Percent Change
Married Couples without Children	26 million	+ 17 %
Married Couples with Children	24 million	– 1
Single-Parent Women	11 million	+ 35
Single-Parent Men	2.5 million	+ 29
Singles Living Alone	22 million	+ 25
Singles Living with Nonrelatives	4 million	+ 46

This means 50 million households contain a married couple, and 39.5 million don't. By the next census, the numbers will be about equal. In 1990, only about one household in four had one or more children of school age.

In addition, the 1990 census showed us the following:

❖ Of our nation's children, 70 percent now have mothers who work outside of the home.

❖ Most of our population now lives in our 39 largest metropolitan areas, mostly in the suburbs.

❖ Of the new jobs created in the decade, 64 percent were in the suburbs. As a result, the most common commute is from a suburban home to a suburban job.

❖ Single-parent women are raising 15 million children at a household income average of $11,400 in 1988 dollars. If there are two parents, the income increases to $32,000.

❖ In the United States in 1990—
  • 13 percent of all children were regularly hungry
  • 25 percent were born to unmarried parents
  • over 20 percent of young children were poor

- about 350,000 children were born to drug-addicted mothers
- 20 percent of our children were not covered by health insurance
- 166 juveniles of every 100,000 were in prison

What Projections Can We Make from the 1990 Census?

Looking out to the year 2000 and beyond, we can project that the total U.S. population will continue to increase—to 267.7 million in 2000 (up 7.1 percent) and to 282.0 million in 2010 (up only 5.3 percent). However, our nation's youth population (age 0-18) will go up from 64 million in 1990 to 65.7 million in 2000; it will then decline to 62.6 million in 2010. This decline is already foreseeable in a decline of females moving into the childbearing years.

Fewer women producing fewer children seems a safe hypothesis. The decline will be in European-American childbearing particularly, as illustrated in the table below:

	1990	2010	Net
European-American youth	45.1 million	41.4 million	−3.7 million
Hispanic-American youth	7.2 million	9.8 million	+2.6 million
African-American youth	10.2 million	11.4 million	1.2 million
Other youth	2.2 million	2.8 million	+ .6 million
Non-European-American net:	up 4.4 million		
European-American net:	down 3.7 million		

"Other" is mainly Asian American and Native American. Calculated from census data and projections.

If the U.S. population continues to grow through the next two decades with youth populations declining after 2000, it is obvious that the nation's average age will go up like a rocket after 2000. The eldest baby-boomers, now 45, will begin to retire in droves after 2000. The baby boomlet is now working its way through junior high, but half of this increase in youth is in California, Texas, and Florida. There is no boomlet in the heartland or in the mid-Atlantic states.

By 2010, the following twelve states plus the District of Columbia will have about half of the nation's 62.6 million young people. The figures below indicate percentages of youth who are not European American in each state:

District of Columbia	93.2%
Hawaii	79.5
New Mexico	76.5
Texas	56.9
California	56.9
Florida	53.4
New York	52.8
Louisiana	50.3
Mississippi	49.9
New Jersey	45.7
Maryland	42.7
Illinois	41.7
South Carolina	40.1
United States (average)	38.2

In these states, a new question arises: can a group be called a "minority" when it represents more than half the population?

We have typically thought of the Deep South as the primary area that includes states with significant non-European-American populations. That was true in 1940, when African Americans were, for all practical purposes, the only statistically significant non-European-American group. Since 1970, the United States has become more ethnically and racially diverse. Many of our largest and most powerful states as well as some states in the Deep South are represented on the list above. In New York, California, Texas, and Florida, each non-European-American group is expanding, beginning with the youngest portion of each group. By 2010, these four states will contain 21 million of the nation's total of 62.6 million youth, that is, one-third of all youth, ages 0-18 in the United States. (New York is a special case;

although youth declined from 4.2 million in 1990 to 3.8 million in 2010, the decline is virtually a European-American decline.) As this majority of young people who are not European American moves through the age ranges, we will see this pattern in this order in these four key states:

- a majority of entry-level workers
- new households
- new parents
- promotions
- voters
- volunteers
- semi-retirees
- non-European-American Social Security recipients

Realistically, it is not likely that the European-American birth rate in the United States (or in Europe) will increase. Given that 70 percent of childbearing-age women are in the work force, deferring having children as long as possible in order to keep two incomes in the family, the notion that vast numbers of women will give up their jobs, return to their homes, and dedicate themselves to the raising of three or more children is fiction—the loss of income would be catastrophic for most households.

Indeed, as non-European Americans enter the middle class, we see a decline in birth rate as well. Middle-class families have by definition some discretionary income, and if that surplus is distributed among eight children, each share will be too small to do much. But if there are only one or two children, the surplus could change their lives.

Several recent reports indicate that around 30 percent of African-American and Hispanic households are middle-income, that is, over $20,000 in 1988 dollars. Asian Americans also have a large middle-income group, due to increased education and multiple-worker households. In Los Angeles, the District of Columbia, Miami, Newark, and Atlanta, a majority of African-American residents lived in the suburbs in 1990, a clear indicator of middle-class membership.

We also need to remember that increased national diversity has brought diversity to those states that typically have not been diverse. Only ten states now have a youth population that is not European American that is less than 10 percent. For example, Maine moves from 2.8 percent youth who are not European American in 1990 to 3.1 percent in 2010, Vermont from 3.8 percent today to 5.4 percent in 2010. Yet, states will become much more unalike in terms of ethnic diversity over the next twenty years, as youth become more concentrated in a smaller number of states. By 2010, 32.2 million of the nation's 62.6 million children will be in only nine states: Texas, California, Florida, New York, Illinois, Georgia, Michigan, Ohio, and Pennsylvania. And even some of these states will have a relatively low degree of ethnic and racial diversity. Pennsylvania, for example, goes from 15.4 percent population that is not European American in 1990 to 18.7 percent in 2010 and Ohio from 16.7 percent to 20.8 percent.

What Are the Implications for Education?

Given that non-European-American groups are more likely to be in poverty than European-American groups, and given our look at the future, we might ask how schools are likely to fare with the clientele we have isolated. The best guess would be that this clientele is to fare reasonably well. Although the conventional wisdom in 1991 was that all schools were terrible, the evidence for that view is very thin. Our nation's best schools are located in the suburbs of our 39 largest metropolitan areas; the worst schools are located in the inner cities of those same metropolitan areas. Some rural schools also fall into this category. We must remember, moreover, that the comparisons of U.S. schools with those of other nations are methodologically flawed, that 31 states actually improved their SAT scores from 1981 to 1991 in verbal, math, or both, and that most national achievement tests have shown no decline over the decade.

However, if suburbs continue to take jobs, income, housing, shopping, restaurants, and corporate headquarters away from their core cities, there is a danger that inner-city schools could become a real socioeconomic dumping ground in the next 20 years. It is also clear from our analysis that states will differ even more in the years to come. Coupled with the amazing changes in the U.S. family over the last decade, early childhood prevention-based programs like Head Start will be even more essential in the future.

We are already beginning to see the power of our largest and most rapidly growing states in areas like textbook adoption as other states watch closely the plans and decisions made by California and Texas in various curriculum areas. Those two states represent one-fifth of all the textbook adoptions in the nation in 1991, and more than one-fifth in 2010. Add Florida to the mix, and you approach one-third. Yet in all three states, the legislatures are not representative of the diversity of the citizens. Neither are the teachers; while over half of all students in these three states will be students who are not European American, about 19 percent of the teaching staff in California, 15 percent in Florida, and 22 percent in Texas will be teachers who are not European American, if you look at who is currently preparing to become teachers in schools of education. These states also have among the highest dropout rates in the nation. Who will assist new European-American teachers in discovering what their diverse students are like?

There is currently a major debate about jobs in the year 2000, but there is no debate about who the entry-level workers will be. (The new workers in 2000 will be an 85 percent combination of immigrants, women, and non-European Americans.) The debate is over the work to be done. Some analysts are insisting that in a high-tech age, most jobs will require a college degree. However, the most authoritative judgment, from an excellent Carnegie study called *America's Choice: High Skills or Low Wages*, postulated that in 2000, 70 percent of our nation's jobs will not require a college degree.

The best guess is that we are creating two work forces. One will consist of minimum-wage occupations such as janitors, clerks, fast-food workers, and hotel-room maids, that can be performed by high-school dropouts. The other will consist of well-paid technical or administrative positions that require a college degree. What has been declining in the United States are jobs in the middle of the economic range. In 1991, for every new job created for a computer programmer, we created eleven new jobs for clerks, or eight jobs for food-service workers, or 6 jobs for janitors. These two sets of predictions concerning jobs for 2000 should make the point:

Fastest Growing Jobs 1988-2000	Percent Increase	Total Jobs in 2000
Paralegal	+75.3	145,000
Medical assistant	+70.0	253,000
Radiologic technician	+66.0	218,000

Largest Number of Jobs, 2000	Total Jobs in 2000
Salesclerks	4,564,000
Janitor-maid	3,450,000
Waiter-waitress	2,337,000

(Monthly Labor Review, November 1989)

Paralegal jobs are growing most rapidly, but the number of jobs is dwarfed by the numbers of low-end service jobs. The service work force has a small middle range and large numbers of high- and low-paying jobs at the extremes.

Given that non-European Americans will constitute such a large percentage of new workers in the next twenty years, there are three possibilities:

1. If more non-European Americans stay in high school and graduate, 1.2 million new health-technology jobs will be waiting.

2. If they drop out of high school, 4.2 million new service jobs will be waiting, of which 3 million are minimum wage (this group is now overrepresented in this job category).

3. If they go to college and graduate, 3.5 million new jobs for lawyers, doctors, teachers, accountants, and so on will be waiting (this group is now underrepresented in these fields).

Our three megastates—Florida, Texas, and California—have one thing in common—tourism is the biggest industry in all three. Tourism hires clerks, waiters and waitresses, and janitors and maids. Most new workers in these three occupations will be workers who are not European American. The equity issues involve access, through education and jobs, to the middle class. It seems unlikely that these three states will be able to increase access to the middle class for their dominant populations during the next twenty years. The result is likely to be social tension over the next twenty years based less on race and ethnicity than on age and class.

It may be time to take the issue of wealth and class head-on as a major focus of our continuing debate about equity. Since the 1960s, we have been devoted to a single equity mission—the racial desegregation of schools. Desegregation of jobs and housing were afterthoughts with daily reminders that the task is not progressing in these areas. But because virtually all non-European Americans (especially African Americans) were poor in 1960, desegregating schools meant equalizing access to the middle class. Today's strategy is different, as many non-European-American households have moved into the middle class. We realize that the young people most at risk of not achieving their potential are young people in poverty, regardless of race. Recent court cases have considered this issue. For example, the courts declared that the Kentucky educational system was unlawful because poor, small school districts were spending much less per child than rich districts. As a result, the Kentucky Education Reform Act resulted. Texas, Virginia, and many other states have also encountered such suits.

The most obvious inequities in 1992 are those of the inner city and its surrounding suburbs. The spending inequities are even more spectacular than those between states. The difference is that there is no governing body designed to deal with the metropolitan areas where most of our people now live. Geographical distance leads to social distance. How do we get wealthy suburbanites to take seriously the problems of the city they fled to get to suburbia in the first place? During the last decade, the wall between city and suburb became even thicker, insulating suburbanites from any real contact with city problems. During the 1990s and beyond, inner-city problems like crime, drugs, poverty, youth violence, family disruption, and social pathology will begin to move past the wall toward the suburbs. At that moment, perhaps, suburban residents will realize that equity is a vital pragmatic goal, that their lives will improve if inner-city residents have access to a good education and a job.

Note on sources: Census materials were gathered from 1990 reports, from CENTADA, the on-line service of the census, and from the 1991 Statistical Abstract of the United States.

Multicultural Education: for Freedom's Sake
by James A. Banks

In *The Dialectic of Freedom,* Maxine Greene (1988) asks, "What does it mean to be a citizen of the free world?" It means, she concludes, having the capacity to choose, the power to act to attain one's purposes, and the ability to help transform a world lived in common with others. An important factor that limits human freedom in a pluralistic society is the cultural encapsulation into which all individuals are socialized. People learn the values, beliefs, and stereotypes of their community cultures. Although these community cultures enable individuals to survive, they also restrict their freedom and ability to make critical choices and to take actions to help reform society.

Education within a pluralistic society should affirm and help students understand their home and community cultures. However, it should also help free them from their cultural boundaries. To create and maintain a civic community that works for the common good, education in a democratic society should help students acquire the knowledge, attitudes, and skills they will need to participate in civic action to make society more equitable and just.

Multicultural education is an education for freedom (Parekh 1986) that is essential in today's ethnically polarized and troubled world. It has evoked a divisive national debate in part because of the divergent views that citizens hold about what constitutes an American identity and about the roots and nature of American civilization. The debate in turn has sparked a power struggle over who should participate in formulating the canon used to shape the curriculum in the nation's schools, colleges, and universities.

The Debate Over the Canon

A chorus of strident voices has launched an orchestrated and widely publicized attack on the movement to infuse content about ethnic groups and women into the school and university curriculum. Much of the current debate over multicultural education has taken place in mass media publications such as *Time* (Gray 1991), *The Wall Street Journal* (Sirkin 1990), rather than in scholarly journals and forums. The Western traditionalists (writers who defend the canon now within the schools and universities) and the multiculturalists rarely engage in reflective dialogue. Rather, scholars on each side of the debate marshal data to support their briefs and ignore facts, interpretations, and perspectives that are inconsistent with their positions and visions of the present and future.

In his recent book, *Illiberal Education*, D'Souza (1991) defends the existing curriculum and structures in higher education while presenting an alarming picture of where multiculturalism is taking the nation. When multiculturalists respond to such criticism, they often fail to describe the important ways in which the multicultural vision is consistent with the democratic ideals of the West and with the heritage of Western civilization. The multicultural literature pays too little attention to the fact that the multicultural education movement emerged out of Western democratic ideals. One of its major aims is to close the gap between the Western democratic ideals of equality and justice and societal practices that contradict those ideals, such as discrimination based on race, gender, and social class.

Because so much of the debate over the canon has taken place in the popular media, which encourages simplistic, sound-byte explanations, the issues related to the curriculum canon have been over-drawn and over-simplified by advocates on both sides. The result is that the debate often generates more heat than light. Various interest groups have been polarized rather than encouraged to exchange ideas that might help us find creative solutions to the problems related to race, ethnicity, gender, and schooling.

As the ethnic texture of the nation deepens, problems related to diversity will intensify rather than diminish. Consequently, we need leaders and educators of good will, from all political and ideological persuasions, to participate in genuine discussions, dialogue, and debates that will help us formulate visionary and workable solutions and enable us to deal creatively with the challenges posed by the increasing diversity in the United States and the world. We must learn how to transform the problems related to racial and ethnic diversity into opportunities and strengths.

Sharing Power

Western traditionalists and multiculturalists must realize that they are entering into debate from different power positions. Western traditionalists hold the balance of power, financial resources, and the top positions in the mass media, in schools, colleges and universities, government, and in the publishing industry. Genuine discussion between the traditionalists and the multiculturalists can take place only when power is placed on the table, negotiated, and shared.

Despite all of the rhetoric about the extent to which Chaucer, Shakespeare, Milton, and other Western writers are threatened by the onslaught of women and writers of color into the curriculum, the reality is that the curriculum in the nation's schools and universities is largely Western in its concepts, paradigms, and content. Concepts such as the Middle Ages and the Renaissance are still used to organize most units in history, literature, and the arts. When content about African and Asian cultures is incorporated into the curriculum, it is usually viewed within the context of European concepts and paradigms. For example, Asian, African, and American histories are often studied under the topic, "The Age of Discovery," which means the time when Europeans first arrived in these continents.

Facing Realities

If they are to achieve a productive dialogue rather than a polarizing debate, both Western traditionalists and the multiculturalists must face some facts. The growing number of people of color in our society and schools constitutes a demographic imperative educators must hear and respond to. The 1990 census indicated that one of every four Americans is a person of color. By the turn of the century, one of every three will be of color (The Commission 1988). Nearly half of the nation's students will be of color by 2020 (Pallas et al. 1989). Although the school and university curriculums remain Western-oriented, this growing number of people of color will increasingly demand to share power in curriculum decision making and in shaping a curriculum canon that reflects their experiences, histories, struggles, and victories.

People of color, women, and other marginalized groups are demanding that their voices, visions, and perspectives be included in the curriculum. They ask that the debt Western civilization owes to Africa, Asia, and indigenous America be acknowledged (Allen 1986, Bernal 1987). The advocates of the Afrocentric curriculum, in sometimes passionate language that reflects a dream long deferred, are merely asking that the cultures of Africa and African-American people be legitimized in the curriculum and that the African contributions to European civilization be acknowledged. People of color and women are also demanding that the facts about their victimization be told, for truth's sake, but also because they need to better understand their conditions so that they and others can work to reform society.

However, these groups must acknowledge that they do not want to eliminate Aristotle and Shakespeare, or Western civilization, from the school curriculum. To reject the West would be to reject important aspects of their own cultural heritages, experiences, and identities. The most important scholarly and literary works written by African Americans, such as works by W.E.B. DuBois, Carter G. Woodson, and Zora Neale Thurston, are expressions of Western cultural experiences. African-American culture resulted from a blending of African cultural characteristics with those of African peoples in the United States.

Reinterpreting Western Civilization

Rather than excluding Western civilization from the curriculum, multiculturalists want a more truthful, complex, and diverse version of the West taught in the schools. They want the curriculum to describe the ways in which African, Asian, and indigenous American cultures have influenced and interacted with Western civilization. They also want schools to discuss not only the diversity and democratic ideals of Western civilization, but also its failures, tensions, dilemmas, and the struggles by various groups in Western societies to realize their dreams against great odds.

We need to deconstruct the myth that the West is homogeneous, that it owes few debts to other world civilizations, and that only privileged and upper-status Europeans and European-American males have been its key actors. Weatherford (1988) describes the debt the West owes to the first Americans. Bernal (1987), Drake (1987), Sertima (1984), and Clarke (1990) marshal considerable amounts of historical and cultural data that describe the ways in which African and Afroasiatic cultures influenced the development of Western civilization. Bernal, for example, presents linguistic and archaeological evidence to substantiate his claim that important parts of Greek civilization (technologies, language, deities, and architecture) originated in ancient Africa.

We should teach students that knowledge is a social construction, that it reflects the perspectives, experiences, and the values of the people and cultures that construct it, and that it is dynamic, changing, and debated among knowledge creators and users (Banks 1991). Rather than keep such knowledge debates as the extent to which African civilizations contributed to Western civilization out of the classroom, teachers should make them an integral part of teaching. The classroom should become a forum in which multicultural debates concerning the construction of knowledge take place. The voices of the Western traditionalists, the multiculturalists, textbook authors, and radical writers should be heard and legitimized in the classroom.

Toward the Democratic Ideal

The fact that multiculturalists want to reformulate and transform the Western canon, not to purge the curriculum of the West, is absent from most of the writings of the Western traditionalists. It doesn't support their argument that Shakespeare, Milton, and Aristotle are endangered. By the same token, the multiculturalists have written little about the intersections of multicultural content and a Western-centric canon, perhaps because they have focused on ways in which the established Western canon should be reconstructed and transformed.

Multicultural education itself is a product of the West. It grew out of a struggle guided by Western ideals for human dignity, equality, and freedom (Parker 1991). Multicultural education is a child of the civil rights movement led by African Americans that was designed to eliminate discrimination in housing, public accommodation, and other areas. The leaders of the civil rights movement, such as Fannie Lou Hamer, Rosa Parks, and Daisy Bates, internalized the American democratic ideal stated in such important United States documents as the Declaration of Independence, the Constitution, and the Bill of Rights. The civil rights leaders of the 1960s and 1970s used the Western ideals of freedom and democracy to justify and legitimize their push for structural inclusion and the end of institutionalized discrimination and racism.

The civil rights movement of the 1960s echoed throughout the United States and the world. Other groups, such as Native Americans and Hispanics, women, and people with disabilities, initiated their own freedom movements. These cultural revitalization movements made demands on a number of institutions. The nation's schools and universities became primary targets for reform, in part because they were important symbols of the structural exclusion that victimized groups experienced, and in part because they were easily accessible.

It would be a serious mistake to interpret these cultural revitalization movements and the educational reforms they gave birth to as a repudiation of the West and Western civilization. The major goals of these movements are full inclusion of the victimized groups into Western institutions and a reform of these institutions so that their practices are more consistent with their democratic ideals. Multicultural education not only arose out of Western traditions and ideals, its major goal is to create a nation-state that actualizes the democratic ideals for all that the Founding Fathers intended for an elite few. Rather than being divisive, as some critics contend, multicultural education is designed to reduce race, class, and gender divisions in the United States and the world.

Given the tremendous social-class and racial cleavages in United States society, it is inaccurate to claim that the study of ethnic diversity will threaten national cohesion. The real threats to national unity—which is an economic, sociological, and psychological sense we have not fully attained but are working toward—are the deepening racial and social-class schisms within United States society. As Wilson (1987) points out in *The Truly Disadvantaged*, the gap between the rich and the poor has grown tremendously in recent years. The social-class schism has occurred not only across racial and ethnic groups, but within these groups. Hence, the rush to the suburbs has not just been a white flight, but has been a flight by the middle class of many hues. As a consequences, low-income African Americans and Hispanics have been left in inner-city communities without the middle-class members of their groups to provide needed leadership and role models. They are more excluded than ever from mainstream American society.

Educating for Freedom

Each of us becomes culturally encapsulated during our socialization in childhood. We accept the assumptions of our own community culture, internalize its values, views of the universe, misconceptions, and stereotypes. Although this is as true for the child socialized within a mainstream culture as it is for the minority child, minority children are usually forced to examine, confront, and question their cultural assumptions when they enter school.

Students who are born and socialized within the mainstream culture of a society rarely have an opportunity to identify, question, and challenge their cultural assumptions, beliefs, values, and perspectives because the school culture usually reinforces those that they learn at home and in their communities. Consequently, mainstream Americans have few opportunities to become free of cultural assumptions and perspectives that are monocultural, that devalue African and Asian cultures, and that stereotype people of color and people who are poor, or who are victimized in other ways. These mainstream Americans often have an inability to function effectively within other American cultures, and lack the ability and motivation to experience and benefit from cross-cultural participation and relationships.

To fully participate in our democratic society, these students and all students need the skills a multicultural education can give them to understand others and to thrive in a rapidly changing, diverse world. Thus, the debate between the Western traditionalists and the multi-culturalists fits well within the tradition of a pluralistic democratic society. Its final result will most likely be not exactly what either side wants, but a synthesized and compromised perspective that will provide a new vision for the nation as we enter the 21st century.

References

Allen, P. G. (1986). *The Sacred Hoop: Recovering the Feminine in American Indian Traditions.* Boston: Beacon Press.

Banks, J. A. (1991). *Teaching Strategies for Ethnic Studies,* 5th ed. Boston: Allyn and Bacon.

Bernal, M. (1987). *The Afroasiatic Roots of Classical Civilization,* Vol. 1: *The Fabrication of Ancient Greece 1785-1985.* London: Free Association Books.

Clarke, J. H. (1990). "African People on My Mind." In *Infusion of African and African American Content in the School Curriculum: Proceedings of the First National Conference,* edited by A. G. Hilliard III, L. Payton-Stewart, and L.O. Williams. Morristown, N.J.: Aaron Press.

The Commission on Minority Participation in Education and American Life. (May 1988). *One-Third of a Nation.* Washington, D.C.: The American Council on Education.

D'Souza, D. (1991). *Illiberal Education: The Politics of Race and Sex on Campus.* New York: The Free Press.

Drake, St. C. (1987). *Black Folk Here and There.* Vol. 1. Los Angeles: Center for Afro-American Studies, University of California.

Gray, P. (July 8, 1991). "Whose America?" *Time* 138: 13-17.

Greene, M. (1988). *The Dialectic of Freedom.* New York: Teachers College Press.

Howe, I. (February 18, 1991). "The Value of the Canon." *The New Republic:* 40-44.

Pallas, A. M.,G. Natriello, E. L. McDill. (June-July 1989). "The Changing Nature of the Disadvantaged Population: Current Dimensions and Future Trends." *Educational Researcher* 18, 1: 2.

Parekh, B. (1986). "The Concept of Multi-Cultural Education." *In Multicultural Education: The Interminable Debate,* edited by S. Modgil, G. K. Verma, K. Mallick, and C. Modgil. Philadelphia: The Falmer Press, pp. 19-31.

Parker, W. P. (1991). "Multicultural Education in Democratic Societies." Paper presented at the annual meeting of the American Educational Research Association, Chicago.

Sirkin, G. (January 18, 1990). "The Multiculturalists Strike Again." *The Wall Street Journal,* p. A14.

Sertima, I. V., ed. (1984). (Ed). *Black Women in Antiquity.* New Brunswick, N.J.: Transaction Books.

Weatherford, J. (1988). *Indian Givers: How the Indians of the Americas Transformed the World.* New York: Fawcett Columbine.

Wilson, W. J. (1987). *The Truly Disadvantaged: The Inner City, the Underclass, and Public Policy.* Chicago: University of Chicago Press.

James A. Banks is Professor of Education and Director of the Center for Multicultural Education at the University of Washington, 122 Miller Hall DQ-12, Seattle, WA 98195.

Reprinted by permission of ASCD from Educational Leadership, December 1991/January 1992.

Part II

REFLECTING DIVERSITY:
A Process

SEXISM

RACISM

CONTEXTUAL INVISIBILITY

OBJECTIONABLE STEREOTYPES

HISTORICAL DISTORTIONS

CONTENT ISSUES

Reflecting Diversity:
A PROCESS

Macmillan/McGraw-Hill School Publishing Company currently works with teams of multicultural consultants in each of the subject areas in which it publishes elementary programs. The first such team was assembled during the development of the 1993 reading/language arts and writing/language arts programs; the criteria by which this team was selected and the processes the team employed during program development have served as a model for assembling other subject-area teams. The following outline describes how the original team was chosen and the contributions it made during program development.

The multicultural consultant team that was assembled to advise us during the development of the 1993 reading/language arts and writing/language arts programs was selected with the following in mind:

❖ The team was to reflect the racial, ethnic, gender, age, and cultural diversity that exists in the United States.

❖ The consultants were to be people whose area of interest or expertise involved bilingual/multicultural education, children's literature, ethnic studies, or cultural schema; published children's authors or poets whose work was reflective of our pluralistic society; or elementary/secondary school people who had served as directors of long-standing multicultural programs or projects.

❖ The team was to be selected in a timely fashion so that it could be directly and significantly involved in the development of the new reading/language arts and writing/language arts programs. That significant and direct involvement would occur early enough in the development of the programs to have an impact on their final form.

To assure the impact on the programs of team input, certain processes were put into place. These processes are described on the following page.

❖ Regular meetings (approximately every other month) were scheduled.

❖ Specific tasks were assigned and subsequently discussed at meetings. These tasks included—

- creating a philosophy that addressed multicultural issues for the programs
- creating a list of statements to articulate how literature could serve as a springboard for discussion of and writing about issues relevant to all children in a pluralistic society, and how literature from a variety of cultures could be compared and contrasted to foster an appreciation for likenesses and differences among them
- reviewing the literature in the program
- creating a checklist to be used during the review of the literature in the program
- creating a review form to be used with the literature review
- discussing with team members in an open forum the criteria used as part of one's literature evaluation
- offering suggestions for selections to be included in the program
- creating questions, activities, and writing prompts to be used with literature selections (to promote thinking and multicultural awareness)
- recommending colleagues who could serve as consultants to help with other subject areas

Members of other product-development teams (social studies, mathematics, science, and music) attended meetings of this multicultural consultant team so that they could see how the process worked and help us identify issues as they relate their content areas.

Reflecting Diversity: Monitoring Apparatus

Appendices A and B on pages 105-108 are samples of checklists developed by the multicultural consultant team that participated in the development of the 1993 reading/language arts and writing/language arts programs. These checklists were created to monitor issues of equity and to assure that sensitivity to certain other issues was maintained.

Sexism:
GENERAL CONTENT GUIDELINES

What is sexism?

Sexism is anything (other than actual reproductive physiology) that defines a person's role in life according to gender; for example, assigning girls and women to subordinate or passive roles or assigning dominant roles and activities to men and boys.

GUIDEPOSTS

❖ That suppression of any group of people threatens the well-being of all will be inherent to the way in which we treat issues of exclusion in our materials. The contributions of women will therefore be evident in these materials.

❖ The fact that more than 50 percent of the population is female will be reflected in the content of artwork, stories, poetry, nonfiction accounts, and examples.

❖ Our materials will not attribute specific traits or values to either sex. We will seek out main characters and figures in history to include in our materials who embody a range of human potential: a rugged woodsman can care for an orphaned animal; a woman can win an important election and display love for her children; a mild-mannered man can act bravely.

❖ Our materials will frequently portray girls and women as active participants in exciting, worthwhile pursuits, and will as often portray males as observers who lend support.

❖ Since more than 50 percent of all married women work outside the home, we will show some mothers involved in outside employment. When at home, women will be shown participating in a variety of activities—reading the paper, paying bills, buildings shelves. We will show some boys and men sharing in domestic chores or as homemakers or as responsible for childcare on a regular basis. Eighty percent of the women who work outside the home do so because they or their families need the money, and because they have skills and training needed in the working world. Therefore, we will not imply in our materials that women's employment is supplemental, unfortunate, or a special privilege. Neither will we discount the value of work within the home.

❖ Because it is a myth that women are always fragile and that men are always strong, our materials will show women and girls as strong, enterprising, competent, and courageous as often as they show males exhibiting those same characteristics. They will also show males to be occasionally self-doubting and in need of reassurance and support.

❖ Our materials will reinforce the notion that tender emotions are characteristic of both sexes.

❖ Our materials will represent women in all professions and phases of employment, including positions of decision making and leadership. Young girls will engage in vigorous physical games, building, inventing, and problem solving. We will take care to show women in tradionally male roles and vice versa.

❖ Since there is no ideal family constellation, our materials will show a realistic variety of family clusters—families with children of only one sex, with older sisters, with one child, with no children, with one parent, with parents of the same sex, extended families, single adults, interracial and interfaith parents. We will take care not to imply that one-parent homes are broken homes or that families that live in houses in the suburbs are perfect.

❖ As females are included in more and more activities traditionally dominated by males, and as males discover satisfaction in so-called women's work, we will strive to support and encourage all human endeavors by both sexes. We will take care to avoid unflattering comparisons between the sexes as well as generalizations about the abilities of either sex.

❖ Unless we are discussing experiences especially related to marriage and children, we will take care to describe men and women apart from marital status.

❖ When discussing past sexism, we will amplify such descriptions with an explanation of the customs, discriminations, and economics involved. This discussion will include the historical forces that created the inequality, how the situation was ameliorated, and the need for continued efforts to make equal opportunity a reality for women. When discussing male-dominated cultures, we will include specific statements about the suppression of women, and describe the contribution—however submerged—of women within the culture. Sexist statements and events may be included in stories and quotations, but they will be cited as examples of attitudes no longer acceptable in our culture.

❖ Our materials will have women speak for themselves and will show women as active forces in human progress.

❖ Our materials will avoid the numbers game of tokenism. Materials will be substantively evenhanded. Issues concerning women will be discussed from the perspective of women as well as from the perspective of men. In addition, issues concerning men will be discussed from the same plurality of perspectives.

Sexism:
LANGUAGE USAGE GUIDELINES

The English language makes it extremely difficult to express oneself in a way that is both grammatically acceptable and nonsexist. However, certain solutions have gained acceptance, and new ones are constantly being devised. Some recommended words and phrases may sound awkward at first, but their use will signal to female readers that they are not being subtly excluded through language.

We consider the following statements and phrases sexist and will not include them in our materials.

- girls (when referring to females over the age of sixteen)
- sissy
- filly (unless you are talking about a female horse)
- tomboy
- You're smart as a man, as strong as a man.
- Women can't... (unless you are referring to the male part of the sex act or growing beards)
- Girls can't...
- bitch (do not use for a female dog)
- He was as weak as a girl.
- Girls are sugar and spice and everything nice.
- That was a manly act of courage.
- He took it like a man.
- Man the sailboats.
- henpecked husband
- ball and chain (referring to a wife)
- She acted like a man.
- He acted like a woman.

The term "lady" (except when referring to the British title) is distasteful to most women because it denotes stereotyped lady-like behavior. We recommend using "woman" and "women." Avoid "men and ladies;" cognate terms are "men and women" or "gentlemen and ladies."

ISSUES	TRY TO AVOID	SUGGESTED ALTERNATIVES
Man: The supposedly generic use of this word implies that all of culture and civilization is the province of the male sex.	man, mankind, men (unless the group is specified as all male)	human, human beings, person(s), people, individuals, humanity, men and women, women and men, figures, personalities
	the rise of man	the rise of civilization, the rise of cultures, the rise of humanity
	great men in history	great figures in history, people who made history
	man's achievements	human achievements
	Cro-Magnon man	Cro-Magnons, Cro-Magnon people
Pronouns: The use of the masculine pronoun in examples omits females, whether or not the exclusion is intended. The converse is true when feminine pronouns are used to describe activity assumed to be female.	The prairie farmer was concerned about the price of his wheat.	Prairie farmers were concerned about the price of wheat.
	Each citizen must pay his taxes.	All citizens must pay taxes. Every citizen must pay taxes.
	The conscientious housekeeper dusts her furniture at least once a week.	The conscientious housekeeper dusts the furniture at least once a week.
	A good nurse cares about her patient's feelings.	Good nurses care about their patients' feelings.
Unless the sex is specified, use "it" to refer to animals	The horse shook his mane.	The colt (stallion, gelding) shook his mane. The horse shook its mane.
	The cat washed herself.	The mother cat washed herself. The cat washed itself.

ISSUES	TRY TO AVOID	SUGGESTED ALTERNATIVES
Pronouns: (cont.) Use "it" to refer to countries and boats.	England ruled the seas. Her navy was huge.	England ruled the seas. Its navy was huge.
The Average Man: In illustrative examples, should include both sexes unless a group has been specifically defined as comprising only one sex.	The average working man saw his paycheck eaten up by inflation.	The average worker's paycheck was eaten up by inflation.
	A typical miner spent a large part of his life underground.	Only males were hired to work in the mines. A typical miner spent a large part of his life underground.
	the man on the street	the average person
	If a man can drive 360 miles in 6 hours, then...	If a person can drive... (or have a balance: "If a woman can drive..." and on the same page "If a man can buy...")
Strong Men/Feeble Women: Do not glorify male exploits while ignoring those of females, or juxtapose trivial events about women with momentous male achievements.	Daring frontiersmen were encouraged by their patient wives.	Daring men and women worked together on new frontiers.
	Abigail Adams was influential in the social life of the capital during her husband's presidency.	Abigail Adams was self-educated and wrote highly intelligent letters. Today these letters are studied by those seeking an understanding of the early days of the American republic.

ISSUES	TRY TO AVOID	SUGGESTED ALTERNATIVES
Women as Baggage: Be careful to avoid language that submerges a woman's identity with that of her husband, father, or son, or that implies that women are passive.	The American colonists brought their wives and children to America.	American colonist families came to America.
	Women were given the vote after the First World War.	Women won the vote after the First World War.
	George Smith married the daughter of John Jones, a rich banker.	George Smith, son of a factory worker, married Brenda Jones, daughter of a rich banker.
	man and wife	husband and wife wife and husband
	Mrs. John Jones	Susan Jones, Ms. Susan Jones, or Mrs. Susan Jones. The trend today is to use whichever title (Ms., Miss, or Mrs.) a woman prefers. However, such titles are not necessary at all.
	John Jones took his wife to California to look for a new house.	John and Susan Jones went to California to look for a new house.
Female Poets and Women Athletes: Sex differentiation is rarely important in the context of a person's work unless you are discussing sex discrimination, or a specific situation in the text makes the person's sex relevant.	sculptress, actress, waitress	sculptor, actor, waiter
	lady or female doctor, scientist, athlete	doctor, scientist, athlete
	suffragette	suffragist
	coed	student
	male nurse	nurse

ISSUES	TRY TO AVOID	SUGGESTED ALTERNATIVES
Sex-Neutral Terms: Revise "man" compounds. Such revisions are usually easier than you might expect.	the working man	the worker
	businessman	business person, entrepreneur, manager, speculator, investor, group leader, trader, business leader
	one-man band one-man show	"Man" is suitable if it is a man; if a woman, say "one-woman show"; if not specified, say "one-person show," "solo performance," or "individual exhibit."
	salesman	salesperson, seller, sales representative
	insurance man	insurance agent
	repairman	repairer, technician
	lineman	line installer
	postman, mailman	postal worker, letter carrier
	fireman	fire fighter
	policeman	police officer
	showman	performer
	spokesman	representative, spokesperson
	chairman	"Man" is suitable if it is a man; if a woman, say "chairwoman"; if not specified, use "chairperson," "moderator," "leader," "group leader," or "chair."

ISSUES	TRY TO AVOID	SUGGESTED ALTERNATIVES
Sex-Neutral Terms: (cont.)	manpower	human energy
	forefathers	precursors, ancestors, founders
	brotherhood	amity, unity, community
	craftsman	craft worker, artisan
	cameraman	photographer, camera operator, camera technician
	man-made	manufactured, simulated, synthetic, hand-built, hand-made, machinemade
	foreman	supervisor
	fisherman	fisher

Sexism:
AVOIDING SEX STEREOTYPES IN ART

Because of their powerful impact on children, visual images provide one of our strongest opportunities to present an unbiased view of people in our society. The following guidelines should be kept in mind as we develop our materials:

❖ Maintain a 50-50 balance between the sexes—numerically and in terms of the significance and prominence of the activity illustrated, within each book and across the series.

❖ Aim for a gender-neutral style of illustration.

❖ Use illustrations that include all physical types, with occasional evidence of physical disability. Avoid stereotypical association of images.

History is replete with instances where women were treated as second-class citizens; current events bear witness to that injustice. We want to depict these conditions clearly in our illustrations. Here is where captions are vital, for they will point out the inequity of the situation being illustrated. For example, beneath a picture of men lined up to vote, the following caption would be appropriate: "The right to participate in the electoral process was restricted to men until the success of the women's suffrage movement in 1920."

ISSUES	STEREOTYPED IMAGES	SUGGESTED ALTERNATIVES
Mother's Role: Don't always show mothers doing housework, cooking, and shopping. Reflect the fact that many mothers are involved in work outside the home and do non-role tasks at home, such as writing, building, and mowing the lawn.	mothers and other females always wearing aprons	males and/or females in aprons when appropriate to the story
	mother sewing while the father reads	the mother working at her desk while the father reads or clears the dining room table
	the mother bringing sandwiches to the father as he fixes the roof	the mother fixing the roof, building a cabinet
	the mother running vacuum cleaner, working at stove, doing wash, carrying food	the father doing household chores independently of or with the mother
	the mother seeing the father off to work	the mother leaving for work carrying briefcase, portfolio, or tools
	the father always driving car on family outings	the mother driving the car much of the time
	the father taking children on adventurous outings	the mother or both parents taking children to the circus, on camping trips, boating, to sporting events
	the mother giving comfort, sympathy, hugs, kisses, hot milk at bedtime	the father being demonstrative and supportive, tending sick child, bandaging hurt knee
	the mother doing the shopping	the father shopping

ISSUES	STEREOTYPED IMAGES	SUGGESTED ALTERNATIVES
Mother's Role: (cont.)	the mother showing shock, horror, fear	the father and mother showing unguarded facial expressions when appropriate to the story
	the father expressionless or relaxed-looking in trying circumstances	the mother more composed than the father
Passive Gestures and Expressions: Watch for the cheerleader syndrome in illustrations. Depict girls in nonrestrictive roles, involved in primary action.	females backing off from the center of action, with males placed more forward (girl recoiling from snake, boy peering down curiously at it)	both sexes participating, with males sometimes in the background (both sexes close to the snake, with perhaps a girl reaching toward it)
	boys playing ball, girls watching	coed teams, boys watching a girls' team play
	females wringing or fluttering their hands; covering their faces or mouths, making warding-off gestures, off-balance poses, or shrinking-back motions, hunching their shoulders, lowering their heads, casting down their eyes, looking as if they are saying "Oh!"	both sexes using gestures expressing confidence and readiness to act, arms frequently outstretched. When required for story line, either sex and/or both may express doubt, fear, imbalance.
	females using coy, flirtatious gestures tilted heads, little shrugs, playing with hair, fingering dress	females and males usually direct in pose and manner; either sex somewhat coy when feeling guilty or asking a favor

ISSUES	STEREOTYPED IMAGES	SUGGESTED ALTERNATIVES
Passive Gestures and Expressions: (cont.)	females usually sitting	both sexes equally active, children are shown sitting only if explicitly so described
Pink Bows and Pinafores: Clothing has long been used to reinforce gender bias. Strive for accuracy, realistic depiction.	girls playing in dresses or always wearing them to school	girls shown wearing appropriate play clothing: jeans, shorts, slacks, sport shirts, T-shirts; school clothing neat, both dresses and pants
	girls always looking cute; wearing frills, ribbons, jewelry	children shown healthy, active—not as ornaments; likely to sport dirt splotches, ponytails fastened with rubber bands. Girls and boys can both appear dressed up in party situations.
	females more preoccupied with their appearance than males; mother at vanity table; girls playing dress-up, buying clothes	both sexes exhibiting reasonable concern for appearance, preening in front of mirror; fathers and mothers using blow-driers, mousse, colognes, and hair sprays; teenage boys cultivating beards; both sexes occasionally buying clothes and trying on adult clothing for fun
	pink for girl babies, blue for boy babies	both colors used together in nurseries, on cribs, baby carriages, clothing; other colors for these situations

ISSUES	STEREOTYPED IMAGES	SUGGESTED ALTERNATIVES
Pink Bows and Pinafores: (cont.)	mothers always in dresses	mothers in slacks, work clothes, dresses, and suits to work and social events
Indoors with Her Dolls: Avoid the environments and standard props used to separate the activities of the sexes.	girls surrounded by dolls, baby carriages, kitchen equipment	girls and boys amid varied objects: tools, chemistry sets, nature collections, books, fishing rods, musical instruments—and dolls
	girls indoors or hovering near doorways, sheltered from the elements, carrying umbrellas when boys are out under the rain	both sexes indoors and out; at play most children are shown outdoors. Include girls in scenes of exploring a new neighborhood, peeking into boats in a harbor, playing in the rain, taking sides in a snowball fight, getting dirty
Women in History: Search for photos and illustrations that show females taking the lead.	pioneer women always cooking, sweeping, spinning wool, rocking babies	women chopping wood, using a plough, carrying bundles of hay, using firearms, helping build a cabin, handling large animals
	pioneer woman riding in covered wagon as man walks	both walking or both riding, or woman walking while the man rides
	lady of the manor doing needlepoint	titled lady riding horseback on estate, checking on crops, issuing orders, signing papers

ISSUES	STEREOTYPED IMAGES	SUGGESTED ALTERNATIVES
Women in History: (cont.)	women selling cakes at a fair	women displaying their art-work or prize animals at a fair
	women as passengers on a sailboat; women sipping hot chocolate in a ski lodge	women hoisting the sails on a boat, participating in a ski race
	women depicted as nurses, elementary-school teachers, clerks, secre-taries, tellers, librarians	women depicted as doc-tors, professors, managers, sitting in a private office with a window and carpet; women police officers, sports figures, construction workers; men depicted in jobs such as nursing, secre-tarial work, waiting on tables in coffee shops. Show men as elementary-school teachers.

Racism:
GENERAL CONTENT GUIDELINES

What is racism?

Racism is the belief that assigns to people an inferior or limited role based on race or skin color, with the assumption that the racial characteristics determine a person's capacities and behavior. The glorification of one race over others, and the consistent exclusion of certain races are also instances of racism.

The anthropological classification of human beings by race—Caucasian, Mongoloid, and Negroid—will not be used in our materials. The terms "racism," "race conflict," and "racial identity" will be used because they acknowledge the continuing struggle of people to overcome bias that is the result of past emphasis on physical differences among groups of people.

GUIDEPOSTS

❖ Our materials will describe the achievements of all people in a similar fashion. They will tell about people of color who created their own opportunities, solutions, and achievements and helped others. We will treat all role models in depth, and we will present persons of color as central, three-dimensional characters in stories and examples.

❖ Our materials will present the realities of history and the present day in terms of such issues as slavery, social brutalization, and poverty so that children may know both the negative and positive aspects of their culture.

❖ To assure that we do not deny the conditions under which persons of color have lived, or sidestep the issue of European American participation in creating those conditions, we shall take care not to present slavery and migrant- and factory-labor exploitation as benign or justified by economic imperatives or other oversimplified explanations. We will not justify expedient treatment of Native Americans by invoking the need for more land and the pioneers' courage in defending themselves against wild savages. Bigots and bigotry must be identified and discussed.

❖ We will not treat prejudice as a given. If a "Whites Only" sign appears over a store entrance, it should be explained, not accepted without comment. Nor should negative emotions in a person of color be ascribed without explanation. All characters should be developed in depth.

❖ Our materials will not espouse a bootstrap approach that guarantees success to the properly motivated, to whomever strives for an education and perseveres, for example, by

(1) doing better, working harder, and cooperating

(2) ignoring insults and wearing the mantle of interminable forgiveness

(3) repressing anger and restraining any show of emotion

(4) being clean and neat

While these virtues may be worthy in themselves, the fact remains that persons of color have had to contend with the discrimination and injustice of oppressive laws that were in some cases instituted specifically to guarantee their failure. All people must be depicted as seeking after good—but not for the sake of placating or appeasing others, overcompensating, or apologizing for themselves. Admonishing children of color, however subtly, to impose upon themselves a paralyzing armor of virtue is only cruel, and again blames the victim for not trying hard enough.

By the same token, we must avoid the implication that people of color cannot make it no matter how hard they try, since the society is so riddled with racism that it is hopeless.

❖ Culture, language, country of ancestral origin, religion, ideals, goals, and morals other than those of the European-American middle-class do not automatically imply lack of advantage, nor certainly do they imply inferiority. Discussing disadvantages as in a teacher's guide, is not synonymous with an inquiry into ethnic origin but is appropriately equated with socioeconomic profile.

❖ Background, setting, and central theme will portray the unique cultural diversity of the United States.

❖ When using materials originating in other countries, especially those that show the cultural roots of our population, we will take care that such materials are authentic. We will be cognizant of the fact that materials about the countries of origin of our citizenry do not substitute for materials about the current development of their lives in this country.

❖ We will show a racial balance in depictions of classrooms, crowds, people on the street, in stores, and in clubs, and at all levels of employment. Persons of color will be depicted within the same socioeconomic range as European Americans. In urban scenes, for a realistic racial mix, about half the people will be people of color. In different urban/suburban/rural neighborhoods, this range may be varied. Our stories will include central characters of color, and a representative percentage of our stories will deal exclusively with people of color—living in the United States. Especially important are stories that reflect values specific to various cultural groups, not necessarily in conformity with European-American middle-class values. Above and beyond such depictions, we will take care to include stories portraying root cultures—African folktales, Mexican stories, and so on—keeping in mind that such stories only begin to fill the need for fair representation of diverse cultural groups in the United States.

Racism:
CONTENT GUIDELINES
FOR SPECIFIC GROUPS

The groups discussed in the following section are groups that make up a significant portion of the U.S. population. They are also groups that have sometimes been underrepresented in educational materials. We want to emphasize that any identifiable group in this country that is presented in our materials will be treated in the spirit described in these guidelines with due regard to proper terminology, their contribution to the culture, and their particular life-style and concerns.

African Americans

Currently, "African American" is the most acceptable term to use when referring to people whose ancestors were born in Africa or who have come to the United States from Africa. Although "black" and "people of color" are terms that are also currently used, we will strive to use "African American" in our materials.

GUIDEPOSTS

❖ Dialects are part of our rich cultural heritage—from southern Appalachia to northern Vermont. Use of the African-American dialect, like the use of all dialects, requires particular attention. Many state guidelines consider dialect a part of our country's rich cultural heritage. Use the following guidelines when considering dialect:

(1) Does it ring true to African-American editors and reviewers?

(2) Is it used to reinforce the myth that African Americans speak a substandard language?

(3) Does it blend in naturally with the story?

(4) Is it in any way demeaning to the user?

(5) If the language African Americans use in a particular story dif fers from that of other characters who are not African Americans, does the difference reinforce stereotypes?

(6) Is the dialect appropriate for the geographical region of the country?

❖ Show African Americans in all communities—urban, suburban, and rural, well-to-do, middle-class, and poor. When discussing urban problems, consider their repercussions on white people as well as on people of color.

❖ Show African Americans engaged in problem-solving activities in business, community, and world affairs. Emphasize self-empower-ment as part of the African-American dynamic.

❖ The strong role of the mother in African-American families stems from ancestral roots in Africa, where women contributed to society on an equal footing with men, and from the days of slavery, when African-American males were often forcibly separated from their wives and children.

   Institutionalized racism has perpetuated the matriarchal role by denying reasonable employment to African-American males. As this historical imbalance is redressed, we should frequently show assertive African-American fathers in African-American family life. At the same time, a balanced view will show the equally important contribu-tion of African-American men and women as parents and as bread-winners, reflecting the role changes now occurring in United States homes in general.

❖ Our materials will show sexual balance within racial or ethnic groups while maintaining the cultural integrity of the group represented.

❖ We will take care to depict African Americans in all professional areas, avoiding stereotyped jobs, and reporting African-American achievements as matter-of-factly as the achievements of any group.

❖ Dr. Martin Luther King, Jr., Harriet Tubman, George Washington Carver, Booker T. Washington, Jackie Robinson—these are important African-American figures, but exclusive concentration on them reveals a preference for African Americans who are acceptable to the

European-American establishment. Additional important African-American personalities will be discussed in depth, including, for example, Paul Robeson, Carter G. Woodson, Henry Tanner, and Paul L. Dunbar, as well as figures such as Nat Turner, Malcolm X, Marcus Garvey, Angela Davis, Jesse Jackson, and Thurgood Marshall, who are considered controversial by some.

Likewise, we will not confine ourselves to the most widely accepted African-American poets or writers, such as Langston Hughes, Gwendolyn Brooks, James Baldwin, Toni Morrison, Alice Walker, or the poets of the Harlem Renaissance: Claude McKay, Countee Cullen, and Arna Bontemps. Attention will also be given to other contemporary African-American poets and writers.

❖ We will take care to discuss African nations as we would European countries. Our materials will reflect the fact that Africa is not a homogeneous, under-developed country inhabited by natives—as outworn images have suggested—but rather a continent comprising many modern countries, each having a unique history, political system, culture, and economy. When discussing Africa's past, we will be accurate and specific about tribal names, practices, artwork, and cultural artifacts and remember that ancient Egypt, with its advanced civilization, was part of Africa. Generally, however, we will not depict Africa only in terms of its past. (Nor do we, except in special circumstances, go to great lengths to describe the life-style of the Saxons or consider them typical of the British.) The focus will be on Africa's emerging nations. Texts will focus on the role played in national and international affairs by modern African political leaders. When South Africa is discussed, its apartheid policy will be described; and the efforts of Africans of color to change that policy.

❖ Caribbean nations, which share a common cultural heritage with Africa will also be represented.

❖ Any treatment of slavery will consider its economic underpinnings but not in a tone that implies its acceptance. The wealth and accomplishments of southern planters will be judiciously taken into account. Discussion of slavery and emancipation will include a consideration of the moral issues involved from an African-American point of view.

❖ The accomplishments of African Americans during the earliest history of this country (prior to the time of slavery) will be recognized in our materials.

Native Americans

The term *Indian*, a misnomer based on Columbus's confusion about where he had landed, has been in use for a long time. While many Native Americans refer to themselves as Indians, it is always preferable to refer to specific groups when you can—Hopi, Iroquois, Zuni, Navajo, for example. ("Native Americans" is the term to use when referring to all such specific groups collectively.)

We must be accurate in identifying the many tribal nations and cultural communities that existed long before Europeans arrived and that exist today. There are numerous confederacies of Native-American nations, with legal provisions and diplomatic protocols. Each group retains its separate identity, customs, and living patterns, and these vary considerably among groups.

The history of Native Americans will be presented as an integral part of the history of the United States. The Native-American point of view, particularly with regard to the invasion of their lands and their subsequent forced removal from them, will provide a balanced perspective and dispel any notion that Columbus discovered an unpopulated America.

GUIDEPOSTS

❖ While we may not be able to describe every single Native-American group, we can be sure to tell and illustrate the history of the groups we do discuss with complete accuracy, making it clear that particular history is unique to a given Native-American group. Native-American culture is extremely diversified and cannot be typified by one Native-American nation or by images perpetuated in Western films. We will take care to use no illustrations or descriptions of early or modern Native-American culture unless they have been properly researched.

❖ The contributions of Native Americans must be integral to our texts, with credit given where it is due. (Recognition of Native-American contributions and achievements usually begins with the introduction of corn to European settlers and, after a long hiatus, concludes with a picture of Maria Tallchief.) Throughout history, Native Americans have contributed to medicine, architecture, religion, philosophy, the arts, sports, and literature. The very foundation that our country is built upon is modeled in part after tenets of the Iroquois Confederacy.

❖ Any descriptions of Native-American spirituality and value systems must be approached with sensitivity. Native-American attitudes toward land and wildlife are being studied today by people searching for answers to environmental problems such as pollution. Many Native-American myths, particularly creation myths, are not quaint folk tales but rather stories with very deep spiritual meaning, and must be dealt with as such.

❖ Textbooks have occasionally glorified the life of Native Americans of previous centuries, either with sentimental descriptions of rain dances or with dramatic—and damaging—portrayals of fierce savagery. Commercial interests have capitalized on a glamorized image of Native Americans in books, movies, advertisements, and even as the names of sports teams. While these images persist in our society, we must take care not to include them in our school materials, perpetuate in any way distortions of Native-American culture by the incorrect use of terms (squaw, papoose, for example), the depiction of cigar store Indians, or stories in which Native Americans speak broken English.

❖ We will take care to establish a historical context when discussing issues of concern to contemporary Native Americans. The history of oppression and current conditions (including those on reservations) will be addressed honestly and from the Native-American point of view. Portrayals of contemporary Native Americans must be accurate—not all Native Americans live on reservations, many Native Americans live east of the Mississippi River. Most Native Americans go to school, hold jobs, shop at supermarkets, and otherwise participate in contemporary culture. On the other hand, Native Americans have their own special life patterns, concerns, and problems, such as a high unemployment rate, a high suicide rate among Native-American teenagers, serious disease problems, and

low average life expectancy. These problems, along with the considerable efforts of Native Americans to find solutions to them, will be
dealt with in our social-studies programs.

Hispanic Americans

The terms "Spanish-speaking Americans" or "Hispanic Americans"
may be used generically, but only when absolutely necessary. Far
preferable are designations relating to the country of origin:

Mexican American
Spanish American
Puerto Rican American
Dominican American
Cuban American

"Latin American" refers to persons now living in Latin America. It,
too, is a generic term; specific designations are far better:

Colombian
Cuban
Panamanian
Peruvian

GUIDEPOSTS

❖ Since Hispanic people live in a variety of neighborhoods and occupy
a variety of socioeconomic levels, our materials will illustrate this.
We will show that many Hispanic people live in the suburbs and in
private rural homes. When discussing Hispanic persons in the context of urban problems or migrant employment, we will present the
economic and social background of these conditions.

❖ The ability to speak two languages is an asset and should be treated
as such. We will take care to show most people of Hispanic origin as
fluent in Spanish and English, or as teaching themselves English. To
reflect the fact that many cities are bilingual, our materials will show
Spanish newspapers, ads, product labels, and other reading materials.
All children, whether speakers of Spanish first or not, can be por-

trayed as curious about Spanish words. To convey to Spanish-speaking readers that stories with Hispanic characters are written for them, not about them, we will not italicize Spanish terms as though they were foreign to the reader.

❖ Our materials will show Hispanic people in a variety of roles with women as well as men working outside the home and in the home, and engaged in a variety of hobbies and other activities. Stereotypically, Hispanic males are depicted as either passive or as supermacho. Females are characterized as passive and obedient. There are some historical precedents for these images, based on cultural values, and these can be mentioned; generally, however, such characterizations fail to include the actual mode of life of Hispanic people.

❖ Care should be taken to avoid misrepresenting the problems of Hispanic Americans. A common stereotype, especially regarding Puerto Rican- and Mexican-American children, is that of the juvenile delinquent or social misfit. This stereotype equates Latin-American descent with criminal tendencies. Spanish-speaking families have their troubles like any other families. Stories about them should center around problems more common than tangles with the law.

❖ As reflective of our society, our materials will depict Hispanic people in all professions with Hispanic children aspiring to careers in all fields.

Asian Americans

The term "Asian American" may be used generically; usually however, we will be discussing individuals or groups from a specific country of origin and can be specific in our terminology:

Chinese American
Japanese American
Korean American
Laotian American
Vietnamese American

The term "Oriental" is no longer acceptable. It is a term coined in the West and does not recognize that Asians are people with distinct histories, cultures, and countries of origin. The appearance, culture, and values of Asian peoples differ greatly, and these differences will be reflected in our materials.

GUIDEPOSTS

❖ Our classroom materials will include Asian Americans in contemporary scenes and as main characters in stories, including those written by Asian Americans. In addition, we may include root-culture materials, such as a Chinese folktale.

❖ Historical events involving Asian Americans and the Asian countries will reflect the Asian perspective as well as the European and European-American point of view. Such events include indentured servitude, racist immigration quotas, the Boxer Rebellion, the reasons Asians emigrated to the United States, the Chinese Exclusion Act, and other laws, and the incarceration of Japanese Americans during World War II.

❖ While Chinese, Korean, and other Asian people do own or work in laundries, restaurants, and grocery markets, they also engage in other kinds of work. We will not rely on stereotypes to depict the life of Chinese or Korean Americans. Like other people, Asian Americans work at a variety of jobs, and our materials will reflect that fact.

❖ Too frequently, stereotypes of Asian women are used to fulfill the vision of the exotic woman or the ideal of delicate, passive, sub-servient, or accommodating womanhood. When discussing Asian customs concerning women, we will be sure that the historical perspective is accurate, not glorified. Today, in the United States and in Asian countries, women work outside the home. Therefore, we must depict Asian women in the same variety of domestic and professional roles as we would other groups of people in contemporary society.

❖ Many Asian Americans are depicted as repressed, studious, goody-goody, mysterious, stoical, and withdrawn. This is a far cry from reality. Asian children, like all children, experience the full range of emotions, misbehave, are not always smart, and are often extroverted. Therefore, if we are discussing cultural traits, we must be accurate and show Asian-American people displaying a variety of characteristics, including prowess in sports, mischievousness, outspokenness, impulsiveness—in a word, human.

Other Groups

Recent immigrants to the United States have come from all corners of the world. People from the Arabic countries of the Middle East, India, Pakistan, Thailand, and countries of Central Asia have come to live in this country. The United States is now home for people from the Pacific Ocean Islands, Afghanistan, Haiti, and many other areas as well. Recent events in the former Soviet Union and Eastern Europe may cause more people from those areas to consider emigration to the United States. As children from these cultures continue to enter our school systems, they must find themselves reflected accurately and appropriately in our instructional materials.

Racism:
AVOIDING RACIAL STEREOTYPES IN ART

Because racial differences are essentially visual, textbook illustrations are crucial. The illustrator and photo researcher must become thoroughly familiar with the spirit expressed in the previous discussion of racism. He or she should study the material to be illustrated for clues to the intent of the story or text and for fresh ideas to replace outworn or stereotypical visual images. Realistic illustrations are critical as we seek to convey the diversity that exists within diversity.

In stylized illustrations, care must be taken to avoid inadvertent caricatures or too much repetition. Color processes that misrepresent skin color must be monitored. Photo studies that show how people from different racial or ethnic groups really look are beneficial. Whenever possible, we will strive to have our materials illustrated by competent, sensitive artists from the racial groups being illustrated.

Equality between the sexes must be maintained. Even when a traditional culture in which women were not allowed to share in many activities is being illustrated, equality can be achieved through numerical balance and selecting for illustration those activities where women played a strong role.

Racial and gender balance will be evident in the artwork, and the series as a whole will reflect this balance.

Illustrations will include all physical types and occasional evidence of physical disabilities.

African Americans

ISSUES	STEREOTYPED IMAGES	SUGGESTED SUBSTITUTES
PHYSICAL APPEARANCE:	African Americans who have white features or all look alike	Artists depicting African Americans must represent a variety of facial features.
	African Americans all having the same skin color	Show realistic variety of skin tones, from blue-black, brown, copper, to very light.
	African Americans with the same hair styles and hair textures	Show natural and sculptured hair styles; vary texture from straight to curly hair.
	drawing styles that exaggerate African-American features	Try to avoid such exaggerations: characters should look natural whether or not the art style is representational.
DRESS:	African Americans always wearing loud colors, straw hats, white suits, exaggerated prints or, conversely, standard, middle-class clothes	Show a variety of styles appropriate to the story line.
	people in Africa wearing native dress or wearing westernized versions of African costumes	Many Africans wear modern dress, particularly in urban areas. Traditional dress is appropriate to some story lines.
ENVIRONMENT:	urban African Americans in crowded tenements on chaotic streets, big bright cars, abandoned buildings with broken windows and	Show urban African Americans living in all city neighborhoods, including luxury apartments, and in suburban houses.

African Americans

ISSUES	STEREOTYPED IMAGES	SUGGESTED SUBSTITUTES
ENVIRONMENT: (cont.)	wash hanging out; or living in innocuous, dull, white picket-fence neighborhoods	When illustrating low-income areas, include a realistic mix of the people living in them.
		When appropriate to the story, do show the action and excitement of city scenes; show, too, the conditions of hardship when the text calls for it.
ACTIVITIES:	African Americans always off the center of action, in the background, watching, helping out	Feature African Americans as the focus of the picture, initiating, performing the action, with persons of other ethnic groups.
	African American depicted as adjunct or foil to the typical voter, average shopper, classroom teacher, the friendly grocer, salesperson	Show persons representing everyday life in the United States as African-American or other nonwhite people.
	one African-American face in a crowd of European-American faces	Show African Americans in racially balanced groups.
	African-American persons used to illustrate lower-level jobs	African-American persons should be represented in all professions, medicine, law, business, education, as well as other areas.

Native Americans

ISSUES	STEREOTYPED IMAGES	SUGGESTED SUBSTITUTES
PHYSICAL APPEARANCE:	long hair, braids, headbands	Traditional Native-American hair styles varied from tribe to tribe. Contemporary Native Americans have a variety of hair styles.
	sameness of facial features, impassive expressions	Study photos to learn how Native Americans really look so you can depict them recognizably without relying on costume props. Features and expressions vary as in all people.
	having red skin	Show realistic variety of skin tones.
	"how" gestures, warlike stances, comic poses	Show realistic variety of gestures.
DRESS:	full headdress, feathers, buffalo robe, war paint, bow and arrow	Contemporary Native Americans wear modern clothing except for special ceremonial occasions.
	women wearing beads, headbands	Ceremonial clothing, which includes very specific, symbolic elements, must be appropriately and accurately presented.
		Traditional clothing and artifacts must be correct for the group as well as the situation being illustrated.

Native Americans

ISSUES	STEREOTYPED IMAGES	SUGGESTED SUBSTITUTES
ENVIRONMENT:	living in tepees surrounded by totem poles and pinto horses with buffalo thundering by	Tribes lived in dwellings that varied considerably—pueblos, hogans, long houses, for example. Many did not have totem poles, did not live anywhere near buffalo, and did not own horses. Be accurate.
	contemporary Native Americans living in shacks on reservations, with outdoor water tanks and bleak landscapes	Many Native Americans live in cities and the suburbs. Show this. Do not play down bad conditions in some reservations when the text calls for it, keeping in mind the Native-American point of view.
ACTIVITIES:	males hunting or in war parties, or passing the peace pipe	Show what males actually did. Some farmed, fished, hunted, or gathered. Each tribe had its own rituals. Do not reflect Western movie images or show Native Americans as always fierce or as killers.

Native Americans

ISSUES	STEREOTYPED IMAGES	SUGGESTED SUBSTITUTES
ACTIVITIES: (cont.)	females sewing buffalo hides, grinding corn, carrying papooses	In some groups, females had (and still have) much status; they comprised the decision-making body, directed farming, building, and political activities. Show this.
	contemporary Native Americans working on ranches or in menial jobs or skyscraper construction	Native Americans are lawyers, teachers, and writers, active in the performing arts, sports, and all other levels of employment. Show them when you are depicting typical employees or representatives of professions.
	Native Americans as marginal creatures of the reservation	Show recognizable Native Americans (use photos to accurately portray Native American features) in everyday life, especially in classroom scenes and family portrayals.

Hispanic Americans

ISSUES	STEREOTYPED IMAGES	SUGGESTED SUBSTITUTES
PHYSICAL APPEARANCE:	sameness in facial features, skin color, size, hair styles, men consistently illustrated with mustaches	Show a realistic variety of physical features and body types; skin color varies from white to very dark; hair can be straight, curly, or blonde. Some Hispanic men do not wear mustaches.
	excessively demonstrative swaggering; women and girls shy and docile	Gestures and attitudes should be appropriate to the story line.
DRESS:	brightly colored clothing; older women in black; girls in dresses	Show modern dress; avoid sexist implications. Be accurate about dress representing indigenous cultures.
	Mexican men wearing ponchos and wide-brimmed hats	
ENVIRONMENT:	Mexican people living in huts	Employ less stereotyped means of depicting original Mexican and other South-American surroundings. African-American and Native-American culture, as well as Spanish, exist in South America.

Hispanic Americans

ISSUES	STEREOTYPED IMAGES	SUGGESTED SUBSTITUTES
ENVIRONMENT: (cont.)	Hispanic Americans either living in squalid sharecropper shacks or crowded tenements	Be realistic about showing harsh conditions when appropriate to the text, but also show Spanish-speaking people in all manner of neighborhoods and environments, including wealthy ones.
ACTIVITIES:	Mexicans grinding corn, riding donkeys	Depict employment of Hispanic Americans accurately, in the United States and in root cultures.
	working at menial jobs as crop pickers, delivery boys, waiters; young people always working on second-hand cars	Represent Hispanic Americans in all professional areas and at all levels.

Asian Americans

ISSUES	STEREOTYPED IMAGES	SUGGESTED SUBSTITUTES
PHYSICAL APPEARANCE:	look-alike features for all ages, for persons from different origins, for individuals within one group; short, skinny, slanted eyes	Study photos to learn realistic variety of face shapes, features, skin tones, eye shapes, height, body size, age characteristics. The use of single slanted lines to depict Asian eyes is never acceptable. Show the individual variety that exists among Chinese, Japanese, Burmese, Malay, and Korean, for example.
	Straight black hair and bangs, buckteeth	Be realistic. Show Asians with straight, wavy, and curly hair, and with varied hair styles.
	modern Chinese males with inscrutable grins, with folded arms or clasped hands, or always wearing glasses and looking serious and polite; mincing, shy women.	Show the full range of human expressions, postures, and gestures.
DRESS:	modern Japanese women wearing kimonos and carrying babies on their backs; Chinese women wearing cheongsam (high-collared) dresses	Even though some Asians—especially older Japanese—do wear traditional attire, show Asians in contemporary dress, except for special occasions in the given country.

Asian Americans

ISSUES	STEREOTYPED IMAGES	SUGGESTED SUBSTITUTES
DRESS: (cont.)	hordes of Japanese with suits and cameras.	Most Asians in the United States are not tourists from Japan. Show variety and individuality.
	modern Asian Americans wearing dark business suits and glasses	Except when illustrating the past, or traditional dress worn on certain occasions, show a variety of contemporary clothing.
ENVIRONMENT:	Chinese people living and working in Chinatowns; in China, in sampans or rice fields	Depict a residential and commercial Chinatown environment when the story calls for it; otherwise, show Asian Americans in the usual variety of neighborhoods and settings, particularly in classroom situations. Be up-to-date in depicting settings in the original countries.
ACTIVITIES:	males as peasants, coolies, waiters, laundry owners, math students	Show the considerable variety of professions held by male and female Asian Americans.
	women as doll-like, infirm, ingratiating to males; geisha girl image	When depicting the root culture search the text for ways to show more than the commonly known roles and rituals.

Asian Americans

ISSUES	STEREOTYPED IMAGES	SUGGESTED SUBSTITUTES
ACTIVITIES: (cont.)	Asian Americans as marginal to representative situations and occupations	Picture Asian Americans in everyday life, in classrooms, and elsewhere.

Contextual Invisibility:
GENERAL CONTENT GUIDELINES

What is contextual invisibility?

Contextual invisibility exists when certain groups, life-styles, or customs are under-represented in curricular materials. Under-representation marginalizes these groups, life-styles, and customs and subtly indicates to students that these groups, life-styles, and customs are of less value, importance, and significance than others.

GUIDEPOSTS

❖ In our materials we will take care to portray our pluralistic society, not a mythical, typical U.S. society. Children should be able to see themselves in our instructional materials.

❖ When presenting the variety of life-styles and customs that exist in our society, we will take care to indicate that all such life-styles and customs are equally valid.

❖ Although the historical context may influence the coverage of certain groups, for example, women, we will take care to determine whether the importance of the group is accurately reflected.

❖ In addition to a balanced portrayal of gender, ethnic, and racial groups, we will take care not to omit or under-represent the physically disabled, the elderly, or groups from a wide variety of socioeconomic or geographical areas.

❖ Balance will be achieved in text as well as in illustrations in our materials.

Objectionable Stereotypes:
GENERAL CONTENT GUIDELINES

What are objectionable stereotypes?

Text and art that generalize about people on the basis of irrelevant characteristics, such as physical appearance, monetary status, age, or special abilities, promotes objectionable stereotypes. Some objectionable examples are dumb athletes; stupid, beautiful women; skinny intellectuals wearing glasses; fat social misfits; old ladies with twenty cats; helpless, saintly, physically challenged persons; narrow-minded working-class people; and exemplary upper classes of bygone days. (Stereotypes that fall into the category of racism or sexism are treated earlier in this document.)

GUIDEPOSTS

❖ Our materials will present the physically and mentally challenged in a wide variety of roles, occupations, and activities, exhibiting to the extent appropriate the following attributes: independence, helpfulness, and diversity.

❖ We will take care to assure that our materials do not perpetuate any of the following stereotypical images of the physically or mentally challenged: helpless, dependent, victims of violence, laughable, or sinister.

❖ Our materials will present the elderly in a variety of roles, occupations, and activities, exhibiting to the extent appropriate the following attributes: competence, independence, helpfulness, and diversity.

❖ We will take care to assure that our materials do not perpetuate any of the following stereotypical images of the elderly: meddlesome, demanding, childish, unattractive, inactive, victims of ridicule and violence.

❖ Our materials will present working-class people in a variety of activities, representing the range that exists in this socioeconomic group in terms of race, ethnicity, neighborhoods, and style of dress, for example.

❖ We will take care to assure that materials do not perpetuate any of the following stereotypical images of the working class: prejudiced, narrow-minded, poor, lazy, intellectually and culturally inferior, childlike, and prone to violence.

Historical Distortions:
GENERAL CONTENT GUIDELINES

What are historical distortions?

Historical distortions occur when materials present only one interpretation of an issue, situation, or group of people. Distortion also occurs when controversial topics are glossed over and discussion of sensitive topics such as discrimination and prejudice are avoided, thereby perpetuating oversimplification and a distorted view of complex issues.

GUIDEPOSTS

❖ Our materials will present information concerning the role and impact of women of a variety of racial and cultural groups on major events in the history of the United States and the world.

❖ We will take care to present information from viewpoints other than a Eurocentric or male one; if more than one viewpoint is presented, we will also take care to include comparable examples and details for each.

❖ Our materials will present the history of the oppressed (for example, those suffering under slavery in the United States) in a manner equivalent to the presentation of the history of the dominant group—for example, from the point of view of the oppressed as expressed in their diaries, speeches, and art.

❖ Our materials will include information relating to social history in addition to political and military history.

❖ We will take care to include difficult periods and events in the history of our nation; for example adequate coverage will be given to the exploitation of workers, repression of union organizers, and anti-strike violence.

❖ Our materials will present working-class individuals as leaders and role models.

Content Issues:
GENERAL DEVELOPMENT GUIDELINES

The purpose of the following section of this document is to discuss issues and opportunities regarding the various groups that comprise our pluralistic society, particularly with regard to specific content areas and materials included in teacher's guides.

Teacher Materials—All Subject Areas

We must make every effort to assure that the authorship teams, consultant groups, and advisory committees that are assembled to develop our programs be reflective of our pluralistic society.

If sexual or racial bias occurs in student materials (for example, a fictional story set during the time of segregation, a historical fiction story that presents women in passive roles, or a presentation of slavery as it existed in the United States), background information in the teacher's guide is crucial. Such information can set a historical context and prompt discussion about stereotypes or sexual or racial bias.

Of course, the teacher's guide materials, annotations, and answers should be written in nonsexist language according to the guideposts stated previously in this document.

Previously published materials will be examined closely at the time of reprint or revision to assure that they adhere to these guideposts.

Reading/Literature/Language Arts

Reading and the literature selections in the student anthologies used for instruction in reading are at the core of elementary-school education. Because of the tremendous potential this curricular area has for shaping children's attitudes, we recommend the following when planning and producing the teacher's guide materials for reading/language arts:

❖ Teacher materials should be sensitive to the inclusion of literary classics in student anthologies. Such classics may include sex-role or ethnic-group stereotyping. These issues should be discussed in the guide.

❖ Care should be taken to discuss female characters who are frequently involved in activities that:
  • are central
  • are highly valued in our culture
  • are outside the home
  • require initiative
  • are active
  • require leadership
  • are physically demanding
  • provide instruction
  • are exciting
  • are fun

❖ Care should also be taken to discuss male characters who are frequently involved in activities that:
  • are secondary
  • are observing
  • are inside the home
  • express emotions
  • show social concern
  • minister to the needs of others
  • show concern for appearance
  • scold

❖ Care should be taken to discuss people of color who are frequently presented:
  • as central characters
  • as significant figures in history and contemporary life in the United States
  • as solving their own problems
  • as initiating important events and helping others solve problems
  • as distinct personalities, having the full range of human problems, emotions, abilities, and aspirations
  • in all professional areas, with emphasis on upward mobility

- in pleasant and varied neighborhood environments
- in recognizable family situations with attention to differences in customs, rituals, and life-styles
- in various social milieus, public events, clubs, special interest groups

❖ Care should be taken to discuss root-culture materials, such as ethnic folk tales, in the proper context, in no way indicating that the people represented in such tales exist somehow in a quaint historical past and not as part of contemporary U.S. society.

❖ Care should be taken to show respect for and an acknowledgment of the richness and beauty of the language patterns of all people.

❖ Care should be taken to allow choice in the selection of topics about which students write.

Social Studies

For cultural reasons, the historical contributions of European-American males have been stressed at the expense of contributions of other groups. Thus, material that is presented for its historical significance or accuracy from the traditional point of view will necessarily reflect an imbalance. Thus, we suggest the following when developing social-studies teacher materials:

❖ Research and amplify the contributions, vocations, and struggles of women and various racial and ethnic groups, discussing them in the course of the text, not just in special sections.

❖ Where people of color and/or women are omitted or bias existed, discuss the situation thoroughly in the teacher's guide in light of today's standards.

❖ Take care to dispel the notion that there is a typical voter, taxpayer, worker, property owner, public speaker, electoral candidate, community leader, doctor, problem-solving parent, child in India, child in France, Colonial child, and so on in terms of gender or race.

❖ An emphasis on the economic need for slaves in the United States oversimplifies slavery and seems to justify it. It is important to represent slavery from the African-American perspective. It must be made clear to students that judged by all present-day standards slavery was wrong. We should convey the fact that slavery was widely accepted in its day, as was the subjugation of women, child labor, the impressment of sailors, and other forms of exploitation that do not exist in comparable form today.

❖ Take care to note that rich, diverse cultures have existed in Africa, Asia, and other non-European areas of the world throughout history.

❖ Include background information about the Native Americans whose diverse cultures existed long before the white settlers arrived so that students can come to understand the Native-American point of view.

❖ Provide background information about the origins of all U.S. residents, their purpose in immigrating, what happened to them, and what their current role is in our culture.

Mathematics

Because the social impact of materials used to teach an abstract subject area, such as mathematics, is less apparent than the impact in literature selections or a social-studies text, special care needs to be taken in teacher materials not to perpetuate any of the stereotypes relating to this subject area—particularly the gender stereotypes. Such stereotyping presents mathematics as a boy's subject and creates a difference in the type of math problem examples that boys and girls solve—for example, the boys solve transportation mileage problems and the girls solve material yardage problems. In addition, we must take care to acknowledge that the body of mathematical knowledge that has evolved over time has been shaped by the contributions from many cultures.

Science

Because of the societal roles that have been traditionally assigned in our culture to women and people of color, white males are credited with most of the significant achievements in science. Thus, women and people of color will be invisible if the text is developed largely as a history of scientific achievements. In light of this the following procedures are recommended:

❖ Research and amplify the scientific achievements of women and people of color.

❖ In discussing the application or significance of a discovery, remember that all people, not just white males, benefit from the discovery.

❖ Consider including in science materials the contributions of people currently working in the field and in related fields so as to be able to acknowledge the place of non-European-American men and women in the field of contemporary science.

Music

While music is, of course, a mental discipline, it is performance-oriented to a considerable degree. In elementary school, the music course is physical: creating (performing), listening, looking. It is, therefore, imperative that activities suggested in the teacher's guide be free from racial and sexual stereotypes. To achieve this goal, authors and editors should bear these points in mind:

❖ With children under the ages of 9 to 10 years, there is no justification for dividing singing groups into boys and girls. This division reinforces any sense that girls and boys may have of being categorized by gender. After boys' voices change, divisions are justified for reasons of vocal range only, not for stereotyping active and passive roles.

❖ There must be no preconceived notions expressed or conveyed about appropriateness of instruments determined by sex or race. Women play brass instruments and larger string instruments; African Americans play strings as well as brasses. Nor do sex and race have anything to do with being a conductor.

❖ In the history of Western musical composition, various groups rightly figure as influences: Africans, Asians, and Spanish-speaking people have all produced music that has influenced contemporary American music and classical music as well. Additionally, women have played significant roles in contemporary and classical choral and popular music as arrangers and composers.

❖ Women and people of color are well represented as composers and performers of contemporary folk music. In tracing this strain of music, authors and editors should be watchful for the roles played by all people. In folk-music literature there is interestingly a significant factor in the anonymous composer. Take care not to presume that person's sex.

❖ Because the language of songs is sometimes sexist or racist or both, care must be taken when selecting them. If a song has lyrics that reinforce stereotypes but is so important historically and musically that it must be included in the program, then the stereotypes must be explained in the text and discussed afterward. Any bias must be acknowledged and explained in a historical context. However, it is wise to keep in mind that young children cannot always comprehend the historical importance of a stereotypical, embarrassing song, no matter what the historical importance may be. Therefore, conducting research to find alternatives is always preferable.

A Word About Illustrators and Photographers

Macmillan/McGraw-Hill commissions hundreds of pieces of art and photographs for the various programs it publishes. Just as these illustrations and photographs should represent the diversity that exists in the United States, so too should the illustrators and photographers themselves reflect that diversity.

Part III

OMAHA PUBLIC SCHOOLS:
Multicultural Nonsexist Education

NEW YORK CITY SCHOOLS:
Guidelines for the Review and Approval of Textbooks

DETROIT PUBLIC SCHOOLS:
Textbook Adoption Policy

MULTICULTURAL INFUSION:
The Dallas Model

Omaha Public Schools:
MULTICULTURAL NONSEXIST EDUCATION

The Reasons

Omaha includes people from many cultural, religious and ethnic groups. It shares a rich tradition enhanced over the years by the cultural history of its people. Children in our schools profit from sharing and knowing about their cultural heritage. They learn to work with others and respect diversity and the interests of their friends and neighbors. As they learn to recognize and change bias and discrimination, our community will become a better place to live.

Goals

As a result of their studies we expect students to reach these goals:

- Develop a positive self-image.
- Develop an understanding of change in society and the ability to cope with it.
- Learn to live in a pluralistic society with mutual respect and appreciation for others.

We are specifically working to help students:

- Respect all people.
- Understand how culture and experience create differences in people.
- Understand that differences in people can be an important benefit to our community.
- Respect the many contributions made by all people to American life.
- Understand and respect their own cultural background as a means of developing self-esteem.

- Develop strategies for dealing with inequities, prejudice, discrimination, and abusive use of power.
- Make personal choices that reduce discrimination, isolation, and prejudice.
- Communicate and work effectively with people irrespective of their race, gender, religion, ethnicity, or cultural background.

Teaching

Exemplary multicultural nonsexist lessons are created by teachers. These lessons are reviewed by community members who represent various ethnic and cultural backgrounds.

Teachers use lessons at every level from pre-kindergarten through grade 12. Each teacher will present approximately 25 lessons per year.

The lessons present the background and history of various ethnic and cultural groups. These lessons focus on the study of culture, the effect of power and prejudice, and the way people of different cultures can communicate.

In addition to these lessons, other events are planned at each school. Guest speakers, musical presentations, recognition of famous Americans, and similar activities are included.

Reprinted by permission of Omaha Public Schools, Department of Instruction and Special Education.

New York City Schools:
GUIDELINES FOR THE REVIEW AND APPROVAL OF TEXTBOOKS

BOARD OF EDUCATION OF THE CITY OF NEW YORK
110 LIVINGSTON STREET, BROOKLYN, NEW YORK 11201
OFFICE OF THE CHIEF EXECUTIVE FOR INSTRUCTION

ISBN & TITLE_____

VENDOR_____ PUBLISHER/PRODUCER _____

LEVEL(S): _____ ELEMENTARY _____ IS/JHS _____ HIGH SCHOOL

TYPE(S): _____ Practice Material _____ Supplementary Text
_____ Student Reference _____ Teacher's Edition/Manual
_____ Other _____

GUIDELINES FOR THE REVIEW AND APPROVAL OF TEXTBOOKS

All textbooks approved for use by the New York City Board of Education should meet the criteria listed below. It is recognized, however, that not every item will apply to each book submitted for approval.

PART A:

Instructions to the Reviewers: Please place a check mark on one of the answer lines next to each statement.

CONTENT

YES NO N/A

__ __ __ 1. The material should promote the objectives related to the course of study.

__ __ __ 2. The material should be accurate, grammatically correct (spelling, usage, punctuation, etc.), conform with standard American usage, and reflect recent scholarship and research.

___ ___ ___ 3. The material should be suited to the interest level, grade level, reading level, and cultural experience of pupils.

___ ___ ___ 4. The material should be comprehensive, of appropriate academic quality, and appropriate for targeted audience.

___ ___ ___ 5. The material should give adequate space and treatment to the role of women in our society and to the changing patterns or characterizations of family life.

___ ___ ___ 6. The material should be free of stereotypical views of any group whether expressed or implied, by statement, visual image, or by omission. The material should be free of any reference, illustration, or characterization that undermines the dignity and status of any class, race, ethnic, religion, age, sex, linguistic, or ability group.

___ ___ ___ 7. The material should avoid unnecessary emphasis on violence and other forms of antisocial behavior.

___ ___ ___ 8. The material should be nondenominational except for books on comparative religions.

___ ___ ___ 9. The material should consider pupil safety and general health. The material should reinforce good health habits, especially related to nutrition, although Advocacy of specific brands of foods or diets should be avoided.

___ ___ ___ 10. Materials should present controversial issues in a manner that recognizes divergent opinions. However, the materials should support those civic and human values guaranteed by our Constitution and that promote good citizenship and foster intergroup harmony

___ ___ ___ 11. Materials should promote the development of students' critical thinking skills.

___ ___ ___ 12. The materials should present cultural, social, economic, and ethnic groups through the use of names, illustrations, and characters to promote the recognition of diversity in our society.

EQUITY

YES NO N/A

___ ___ ___ 1. The contributions of all cultural, linguistic, racial, and ethnic groups to our society should be appropriately integrated in the relevant place and period.

___ ___ ___ 2. Materials should be presented from a nonethnocentric perspective and where possible historical events should be viewed from a variety of perspectives.

ORGANIZATION

YES NO N/A

__ __ __ 1. The table of contents and the index should be complete and arranged so that information may be easily found.

__ __ __ 2. There should be a glossary that gives the pronunciation and meaning of unusual and difficult words.

__ __ __ 3. Charts, maps, tables, graphs, and illustrations should be presented clearly.

__ __ __ 4. Where appropriate, there should be thought-provoking summaries and reviews at the end of each unit.

__ __ __ 5. The suggested related activities—study helps, suggested readings, pupil and teacher activities, etc.—should foster further development of knowledge, attitudes, and/or appreciation.

__ __ __ 6. There should be a list of recommended reference books.

__ __ __ 7. Material should be free of advertising

__ __ __ 8. Commercial products pictured may be appropriate if they are relevant to the grade level and are presented in good taste.

TECHNICAL QUALITY

YES NO N/A

__ __ __ 1. Print size should be appropriate to grade level.

__ __ __ 2. Illustrations should be artistic, attractive, well located on the page, and suitable in type for the grade.

__ __ __ 3. Textbook binding should be sufficiently sturdy to withstand normal handling by students.

__ __ __ 4. Paper should be of sufficient quality so that print marks do not show through.

__ __ __ 5. Materials should be presented with consideration of the varied learning styles of students.

__ __ __ 6. Reproductions of artwork or other outside resource materials should be of significantly high quality so as not to detract from original.

PART C: Evaluation Decision

Instructions to the Reviewers: Following the completion of your review you are to complete the following section of the <u>Submittal Form for Textbooks and Ancillary Materials</u> for this product.

_____ Instructional Materials Approved

_____ Instructional Material Disapproved (If <u>disapproved</u>, complete in detail on the attached form, Part B, your reasons for disapproval).

_____   _____

(Date)   Reviewer's Signature

_____   _____

(Date)   Reviewer's Signature

Reprinted with permission from *Guidelines for the Review and Approval of Textbooks* of the Board of Education of the City of New York.

Detroit Public Schools:
TEXTBOOK ADOPTION POLICY

The Detroit Board of Education has had a published textbook adoption policy since July 1968.

Beginning October, 1991 the policy for textbook adoptions will be revised to include criteria for multicultural content in textbooks and other learning materials. Embedded in the criteria is the present Board policy related to the treatment of race and sex in textbooks.

Multicultural/Multiethnic Definition

Multicultural/Multiethnic Education is an ongoing process that prepares people to value diversity and view cultural differences as a positive and vital force in the continued development of society. This process prepares people to live, learn, and work in a pluralistic world. It promotes respect for the intrinsic worth of each individual regardless of ethnicity, race, religion, sex, socioeconomic, physical, or mental condition and must be an essential part of the educational process.

Criteria for Content and Other Learning Material Appropriate for Use in the Detroit Public Schools

Textbooks and learning materials selected for use will meet or exceed the quality standards currently used in the textbook selection process and the additional criteria listed below.

1. Content and learning materials will be screened for **Truth** as defined by:

   _____ Content that can be documented and defended using primary sources wherever possible;

   _____ The availability of bibliographies and other source materials;

   _____ Inclusiveness of content that is known and documented but traditionally omitted through negligence or design;

_____ Content free of distortions such as misrepresentations, errors, oversimplifications, and erroneous attributions and conclusions;

_____ The use of photographs instead of artist renderings where possible;

_____ Charts, diagrams, photographs, illustrations, and side bars that enhance content and support truth;

_____ Maps that show proportional land mass and explain the difference between natural and political geography;

_____ Authors and contributors with extensive knowledge/ credentials and experience in the field and proven sensitivity to the group or subject involved.

2. Content and learning materials will be screened for **Balance**; meaning the material will be:

_____ Infused with the concepts underlying multiculturalism such as the oneness of humanity and interdependence and inter-relatedness of cultural and ethnic groups;

_____ Free of excesses, extremes, exaggerations, incomplete thoughts, and unqualified half-truths;

_____ Reflective of different view points that encourage and foster critical thinking;

_____ Diverse with instructional strategies;

_____ Contextually balanced with regards to illustrations and portrayals of various cultural and ethnic groups.

3. Content and learning materials will be screened for **Order** and thus have:

_____ Historical order and sequence that reflects the universal development of cultures and ethnic groups;

_____ Parallel chronological events reported in perspective;

_____ Topics and concepts treated in sufficient depth to enhance understanding;

_____ Examples that are relevant, meaningful to the given curriculum content, and illustrative of principles, generalizations, and theories;

_____ No evidence of propaganda or hidden purpose.

4. Content and learning materials will be screened for **Harmony** in that:

_____ Words, names, and views used are the same as those used by the subject group, i.e., call people what they call themselves;

_____ Positive, harmonist, human events are used as historical and/or relevant guideposts;

_____ Materials are written from the perspective of the group(s) being discussed;

_____ There is inclusion of various perspectives and significant examples of folklore, customs, symbols and practices related to the topics.

5. Content and learning materials must be **Bias free and Multicultural** in that there is:

_____ No overrepresentation

_____ No underrepresentation

_____ No stereotyping

_____ No deliberate selectivity of content

_____ No glossing over of issues

_____ No deliberate isolation and fragmentation

_____ No discriminatory language

_____ No marginalizing of contributions

Multicultural Infusion:
THE DALLAS MODEL—A Collage of Cultures
DALLAS INDEPENDENT SCHOOL DISTRICT, DALLAS, TEXAS

Premises

- Conflicts develop whenever groups with diverse cultures interact.
- Diversity enriches a society and provides novel ways to view events and situations and to solve problems.
- All schools, especially Dallas Independent School District (DISD), today must shape a modernized, national culture that has selected aspects of traditional culture coexisting in a balance with a modernized, post industrial society.
- The DISD multicultural curricula should change the basic assumption about what "American" means and to present students with new ways of viewing and interpreting American society, literature, music, art, mathematics, science, and all other disciplines.
- The DISD multicultural infusion curricula should help students develop cross-cultural competency—the ability to function within a range of cultures.
- Students must have a sophisticated understanding of the nature of race and ethnicity in their society in order to become literate and fully effective citizens.
- Curricula that teaches only mainstream views and perspectives gives students a distorted and incomplete view of their nation and the world.
- The major goal of the DISD multicultural infusion curricula is to help students develop decision-making skills so that they become effective change agents in contemporary society.
- To help DISD students to develop effective decision-making skills and to take appropriate accompanying social action, the multicultural infusion curricula must provide opportunities to master higher-level concepts and generalizations.

Part IV

BIBLIOGRAPHY

MULTICULTURAL INFORMATION SOURCES

AUTHORS AND ILLUSTRATORS
FROM SPECIFIC GROUPS

Bibliography

Allport, Gordon. *The Nature of Prejudice.* Garden City, N.Y.: Doubleday Anchor Books, 1958.

Anson, Robert Sam. *Best Intentions: The Education and Killing of Edmund Perry.* New York: Random House, 1987.

Appleton, Nicholas. *Cultural Pluralism in Education: Theoretical Foundations.* New York: Longman, 1983.

Archdeacon, Thomas J. *Becoming American: An Ethnic History.* New York: The Free Press, 1983.

Baker, Gwendolyn. *Planning and Organizing for Multicultural Instruction.* New York: Addison-Wesley Publishing Company, 1983.

Banks, James. *Teaching Strategies for Ethnic Studies.* 4th ed. Boston: Allyn and Bacon, 1987.

Multiethnic Education: Theory and Practice. 2nd ed. Boston: Allyn and Bacon, 1988.

Banks, James, and Banks, Cherry A. McGee. *Multicultural Education: Issues and Perspectives.* Boston: Allyn and Bacon, 1989.

Bennett, C.I. *Comprehensive Multicultural Education.* Boston: Allyn and Bacon, 1986.

Chen, Jack. *The Chinese of America.* New York: Harper and Row, 1980.

Choy, Bong-youn. *Koreans in America.* Chicago: Nelson-Hall, 1979.

Fitzgerald, J. P. *Puerto Rican Americans: The Meaning of Migration to the Mainland.* Englewood Cliffs, N.J.: Prentice-Hall, 1981.

Garcia, R. L. *Teaching in a Pluralistic Society: Concepts, Models, Strategies.* New York: Harper & Row, 1982.

Gibbs, Jewelle Taylor, and Huang, Larke Nahme. *Children of Color.* San Francisco: Jossey-Bass Publishers, 1989.

Gollnick, Donna, and Chinn, Philip C. *Multicultural Education in a Pluralistic Society.* Columbus, Ohio: Merrill, 1986.

Goodlad, J.I. *A Place Called School*. New York: McGraw-Hill, 1984.

Goodman, M.E. *Race Awareness in Young Children*. Cambridge, MA: Addison-Wesley, 1952.

Haines, David W., ed. *Refugees as Immigrants: Cambodians, Laotians, and Vietnamese in America*. New York: Rowman and Littlefield Publishers, 1989.

Hernandez, Hilda. *Multicultural Education: A Teacher's Guide to Content and Processes*. Columbus, Ohio: Merrill, 1989.

Higham, John, ed. *Ethnic Leadership in America*. Baltimore: Johns Hopkins University Press, 1978.

Hochschild, Jennifer L. *The New American Dilemma*. New Haven: Yale University Press, 1984.

Kimball, S.T. *Diversity in the Classroom*. New York: Teachers College Press, 1983.

Kitano, Harry, and Dailies, Roger. *Asian-Americans: Emerging Minorities*. Englewood Cliffs, N.J.: Prentice-Hall, 1988.

Kranz, Rachel. *The Biographical Dictionary of Black America*. New York: Facts on File, 1992.

Lynch, James. *Multicultural Education: Principles and Practice*. Boston: Routledge and Kegan Paul, 1986.

Milner, David. *Children and Race*. Beverly Hills: Sage Publications, 1983.

Murray, Charles. *Losing Ground: American Social Policy 1950-1980*. New York: Basic Books, 1984.

Oakes, Jeannie. *Keeping Track: How Schools Structure Inequality*. New Haven: Yale University Press, 1985.

Peterson, William, Novak, Michael, and Gleason, Philip. *Concepts of Ethnicity*. Cambridge, MA: Harvard University Press, 1982.

Perlman, Joel. *Ethnic Differences, Schooling and Social Structure Among the Irish, Italians, Jews and Blacks in an American City 1880-1935*. Cambridge Mass.: Harvard University Press, 1988.

Ramirez, Arnulfo. *Bilingualism Through Schooling*. Albany: State of New York University Press, 1985.

Ramirez, M. and Castaneda, A. *Cultural Democracy, Bicognitive Development, and Education*. New York: Academic Press, 1976.

Ramsey, Patricia C. *Teaching and Learning in a Diverse World*. New York: Teachers College Press, 1987.

Ravitch, Diane. *The Troubled Crusade*. New York: Basic Books, 1983.

Sadker, M. and Sadker, A. *Sex Equity Handbook for Schools*. New York: Longman, 1982.

Sale, Kirkpatrick. *The Conquest of Paradise*. New York: Penguin, 1990.

Spicer, Edward H. *The American Indians*. Cambridge, MA: Harvard University Press, 1982.

Strand, Paul J., and Jones, Woodrow, Jr. *Indochinese Refugees in America: Problems of Adaptation and Assimiliation*. Durham, N.C.: Duke University Press, 1985.

Weis, Lois, ed. *Class, Race, and Gender in American Education*. Albany: State University of New York Press, 1988.

Wilson, Robert A., and Hosokawa, Bill. *East to America: A History of the Japanese in the United States*. New York: William Morrow, 1980.

Wilson, William J. *The Truly Disadvantaged: The Inner City, the Underclass and Public Policy*. Chicago: University of Chicago Press, 1987.

Multicultural Information Sources

The following resources are provided as references for authors, editors, and illustrators as they develop materials about specific groups. Please note that this list is by no means all-inclusive.

African-American Resources

Alternative Videos
837 Exposition Avenue
Dallas, Texas 75226
(214) 823-6030

African-American Culture & Arts Network, Inc.
2090 Adam Clayton Powell Boulevard
New York, New York 10031
(212) 749-4408
(800) 439-6262

Afro-American History and Cultures Exhibit
Anacostia Neighborhood Museum
Smithsonian Institute
1921 Fort Place, S.E.
Washington, D.C. 20020
(202) 287-3306

National Museum of African Art
Smithsonian Institute
950 Independence Avenue, S.W.
Washington, D.C. 20560
(202) 357-4600

American Visions
Visions Foundation, Inc.
Carter G. Woodson House
1538 Ninth Street, N.W.
Washington, D.C. 20001
(202) 462-1779

Association for the Study of Afro-American Life & History
140 12th Street, N.W.
Washington, D.C. 20005
(202) 667-2822

DuSable Museum
57th and Cottage Grove
Chicago, Illinois 60637
(312) 947-0600

Midwest Desegregation Center
401 Bluemont Hall
Kansas State University
Manhattan, Kansas 66506
(913) 532-6408

Museum of Afro-American History
Box 5
Boston, Massachusetts 02119
(617) 742-1852

Schomburg Center for Research in Black Culture
515 Malcolm X Boulevard
New York, New York 10037
(212) 491-2200

Studio Museum in Harlem
144 West 125th Street
New York, New York 10027
(212) 864-4500

Asian-American Resources

Arthur M. Sackler Gallery
1050 Independence Avenue, S.W.
Washington, D.C. 20560
(202) 357-1300

Asia Society
725 Park Avenue
New York, New York 10021
(212) 288-6400

**Asian and Pacific American
 Chamber of Commerce**
1112 Carper Street
McLean, VA 22101
(202) 659-4037

**Asian and Pacific Island Curricular
 Materials and Professional
 Development Materials
Evaluation, Dissemination and
 Assessment Center**
California State University, Los Angeles
5151 State University Drive
Los Angeles, California 90032

**Bureau of East Asia and
 Pacific Affairs,
Department of State Public Affairs,**
Room 5310 2201 C Street, N.W.
Washington, D.C. 20520
(202) 647-2538

Embassy of Japan
2520 Massachusetts Avenue, N.W.
Washington, D.C. 20008
(202) 234-2266

Japan Society
333 E. 47th Street
New York, New York 10017
(212) 832-1155

Korean Information Service
14134 22nd Street, N.W.
Washington, D.C. 20037
(202) 296-4256

Library of Congress, Asian Division
Washington, D.C. 20540
(202) 287-5420

Oriental Library
University of California at Los Angeles,
Room 21617 Research Library
Los Angeles, California 90014

Pacific Asia Museum
46 N. Los Robles
Pasadena, California 91101
(818) 449-2742

The East-West Center
1777 East-West Road
Honolulu, Hawaii 96848
(808) 944-7204

Hispanic-American Resources

**American Academy of Arts
  and Letters**
633 West 155th Street
New York, New York 10032
(212) 368-5900

Center for Inter-American Relations
680 Park Avenue
New York, New York 10021
(212) 249-8950

**Central American in the Classroom
Network of Educators on Central America**
1118 22nd Street, N.W.
Washington, D.C. 20037
(202) 429-0137

Council on Hemispheric Affairs (COHA)
1900 L Street, N.W., Suite 201
Washington, D.C. 20036
(202) 775-0216

Embassy of Mexico
2829 16th Street, N.W.
Washington, D.C. 20009
(202) 234-6000

Embassy of Panama
2862 McGill Terrace, N.W.
Washington, D.C. 20008
(202) 483-1407

Embassy of Peru
1700 Massachusetts Avenue, N.W.
Washington, D.C. 20036
(202) 833-9860

Embassy of Spain
2700 15th Street, N.W.
Washington, D.C. 20009
(202) 265-1084

**Hispanic Magazine
Hispanic Publishing Corporation**
111 Massachusetts Avenue, N.W. Suite 410
Washington, D.C. 20001

Hispanic Society
613 West 155th Street
New York, New York 10032
(212) 690-0743

**Information Services on
  Latin America (ISLA)**
464 19th Street
Oakland, California 94612
(415) 835-0678

**Library of Congress,
  Hispanic Division**
Room 239E
Washington, D.C. 20540
(202) 287-5420

Museo del Barrio
1230 5th Avenue
New York, New York 10029
(212) 831-7272

**Pan American Institute of
  Geography and History**
Ex-arzobispado 29
Col. Observatorio, Mexico 11860
2-77-58-88

Washington Office on Latin America
110 Maryland Avenue, N.E.
Washington, D.C. 20002
(202) 544-8045

Native-American Resources

Alaska Native Arts and Crafts Center of Fairbanks, Alaska
1603 College Road
Fairbanks, AK 99701
(907) 456-2323

American Indian Archaeological Institute
Curtis Road, off Route 199
P.O. Box 260
Washington, CT 06793
(203) 868-0518

American Indian Community House
404 Lafayette Street
New York, NY 10003
(212) 598-0100

Center of the American Indian
2100 Northeast 52nd Street
Kirkpatrick Center
Oklahoma City, OK 73111
(405) 427-5461

Cherokee National Museum (Heritage Center)
P.O. Box 515
Tahlequah, OK 74464
(918) 456-6007

Chickasaw Council House Museum
Court House Square, P.O. Box 717
Tishomingo, OK 73460
(405) 371-3351

Choctaw Council House Historical Museum
Route 1, Box 105-3A
Tuskohoma, OK 74574
(918) 569-4465

Creek Council House and Museum
Town Square
Okmulgee, OK 74447
(918) 756-2324

Eight Northern Pueblo Indian Artisans Guild
P.O. Box 1079
San Juan Pueblo, NM 87566
(505) 852-4283

Field Museum of Natural History
Roosevelt Road at Lake Shore Drive
Chicago, IL 60505
(312) 922-9410

The Five Civilized Tribes Museum
Agency Hill, Honor Heights Drive
Muskogee, OK 74401
(918) 683-1701

Indian Pueblo Cultural Center, Inc.
2401 12th Street NW
Albuquerque, NM 87102
(505) 843-7270 or 843-7271

Iroquois Indian Museum
Box 158 N. Main Street, Dept. DB
Schoharie, NY 12157
(518) 295-8553

Kiowa Tribal Museum
P.O. Box 369
Carnegie, OK 73015
(405) 654-2300

Makah Cultural and Research Center
P.O. Box 95
Neah Bay, WA 98357
(206) 645-2711

Native-American Resources

Makah Cultural and Research Center
P.O. Box 95
Neah Bay, WA 98357
(206) 645-2711

Mescalero Apache Cultural Center
P.O. Box 175
Mescalero, NM 88340
(505) 671-4495

**Mound City Group
    National Monument**
16062 State Route 104
Chillicothe, OH 45601
(614) 774-1125

Museum of the American Indian
Heye Foundation
155th Street and Broadway
New York, NY 10032
(212) 283-2420

Museum of the Cherokee Indian
U.S. Highway 441 North
P.O. Box 770-A
Cherokee, NC 28719
(704) 497-3481

Museum of Indian Heritage
6040 De Long Road
Eagle Creek Park
Indianapolis, IN 46254
(317) 293-4488

Museum of Native American Culture
East 200 Cataldo Street
Spokane, WA 99220
(509) 326-4550

**Museum of the Plains Indians and
    Craft Center**
P.O. Box 400
Browning, MT 59417
(406) 338-2230

Navajo Tribal Museum
Box 308, Highway 264
Window Rock, AZ 86515
(602) 871-6673 & 6675

Osage Tribal Museum
Osage Agency Campus, Grandview Ave.
Pawhuska, OK 74056
(918) 287-2495, ext. 280

Pueblo Grande Museum
4619 East Washington Street
Phoenix, AZ 85034
(602) 275-3452

Seminole Nation Museum
P.O. Box 1532
524 South Wewoka Avenue
Wewoka, OK 74884
(405) 257-5580

Seneca-Iroquois National Museum
P.O. Box 442, Broad Street Extension
Salamanca, NY 14779
(716) 945-1738

Sioux Indian Museum
Box 1504
Rapid City, SD 57709
(605)348-0557 or 8834

Native-American Resources

Society for American Indian Studies and Research
P.O. Box 443
Hurst, TX 76053
(817) 281-3784

Southeast Alaska Indian Culture Center
P.O. Box 944
Sitka, AK 99835
(907) 747-6281

Southern Plains Indian Museum
Box 749
Anadarko, OK 73005
(405) 247-6221

Southwestern Association on Indian Affairs, Inc.
La Fonda Hotel
Santa Fe, NM 87501
(505) 983-5220

United Indians of All Tribes Foundation Daybreak Star Arts Center
Discovery Park
P.O. Box 99253
Seattle, WA 98199
(206) 285-4425

University of British Columbia Museum of Anthropology
6393 Northwest Marine Drive
Vancouver, BC V6T 1W5
(604) 228-3825 (taped message)
(604) 228-5087 (business)

University of California
Robert H. Lowie Museum of Anthropology
103 Kroeber Hall
Berkeley, CA 94720
(415) 642-3681

Wheelwright Museum of the American Indian
704 Camino Lejo
Box 5153
Santa Fe, NM 87502
(505) 982-4636

General Multicultural Resources

Claudia's Caravan
P.O. Box 1582
Alameda, California 94501
(510) 521-7871

Balch Institute for Ethnic Studies
18 S. 7th Street
Philadelphia, Pennsylvania 19106
(215) 925-8292

**Appalachia Educational Laboratory
ERIC Clearinghouse for Rural and
   Small Schools**
P.O. Box 1348 Charleston,
West Virginia 25325
(800) 624-9120

**CHIME/National Center for
   Immigrant Students**
100 Boylston Street, #737
Boston, Massachusetts 02116
(800) 441-7192
(617) 357-8507

Ethnic Materials Information Exchange Task
Force 68-78 Bell Boulevard
Bayside, New York 11364
(212) 229-1510 or (212) 520-7194

Evaluation Assistance Center-West/NMHU
Springer Square Building
121 Tijeras N.E., Suite 2100
Albuquerque, New Mexico 87102
(800) 247-4269

Immigration History Society
690 Cedar Street
St. Paul, Minnesota 55101

Information Center on Children's Cultures
331 East 38th Street
New York, New York 10016
(212) 686-5522

**Multicultural Review
Greenwood Publishing Group**
88 Post Road West Box 5007
Westport, Connecticut 06881-5007

National Association of Bilingual Education
810 1st Street, N.E., 3rd Floor
Washington, D.C. 20002
(202) 898-1829

National Geographic Traveler
P.O. Box 37054
Washington, DC 20036
(202) 828-5485

Society for Ethnomusicology
Box 2984
Ann Arbor, Michigan 15106
(313) 663-1947

**Southwest Educational
   Development Laboratory**
211 East 7th Street
Austin, Texas 78701
(512) 476-6861

Smithsonian Institution
100 Jefferson Drive SW
Washington, DC 20560
(202) 357-1300

Authors and Illustrators
FROM SPECIFIC GROUPS

This list of names is by no means all-inclusive. These are authors and illustrators with whom we at Macmillan/McGraw-Hill have had an opportunity to work. A particular racial/national background is not necessary for the creation of a children's book on any theme or topic.

African/African-American

Bearden, Romare, *author*
Bishop, Rudine Sims (See: Sims), *author*
Boyd, Candy Dawson, *author*
Brooks, Gwendolyn, *author*
Bryan, Ashley, *author/illustrator*
Byard, Carole, *illustrator*
Caines, Jeannette Franklin, *author*
Casilla, Robert, *illustrator*
Childress, Alice, *author*
Chocolate, Deborah Newton, *author/illustrator*
Clifton, Lucille, *author*
Cooper, Floyd, *illustrator*
Cummings, Pat, *author/illustrator*
Davis, Ossie, *author*
Dillon, Leo, *author/illustrator*
Diop, Birago, *author*
Feelings, Tom, *author/illustrator*
Ferguson, Mr. Amos, *illustrator*
Fields, Julia, *author*
Flournoy, Valerie R., *author*
Ford, Bernette G., *author*
Ford, George, *illustrator*
Gilchrist, Jan Spivey, *illustrator*
Giovanni, Nikki, *author*
Greenfield, Eloise, *author*
Guy, Rosa, *author*
Hamilton, Virginia, *author*

Hanna, Cheryl, *illustrator*
Haskins, James, *author*
Howard, Elizabeth Fitzgerald, *author*
Hudson, Cheryl Willis, *illustrator*
Hudson, Wade, *author*
Hughes, Langston, *author*
Johnson, Angela, *author*
King, Coretta Scott, *author*
Lester, Julius, *author*
Little, Lessie Jones, *author*
Mattox, Cheryl Warren, *author*
McKissack, Fredrick, *author*
McKissack, Patricia, *author*
Myers, Walter Dean, *author*
Pate, Rodney, *illustrator*
Pinkney, J. Brian, *author/illustrator*
Pinkney, Jerry, *illustrator*
Ransome, James E., *illustrator*
Rosales, Melodye, *illustrator*
Sims, Rudine, *author*
Steptoe, John, *author*
Strickland, Dorothy S., *author*
Taylor, Mildred D., *author*
Walker, Alice, *author*
Walter, Mildred Pitts, *author*
Ward, John, *illustrator*

Native-American

Begay, Shonto, *illustrator*
Carter, Forrest, *author*
Ekoomiak, Normee, *author/illustrator*
Sneve, Virginia Driving Hawk, *author*

Te Ata, *story teller*
Trafzer, Cliff, *author*
Vizenor, Gerald, *author*
Yellow Robe, Rosebud, *author*

Asian-American

Anno, Mitsumasa, *author/illustrator*
Chang, Heidi, *illustrator*
Kingston, Maxine Hong, *author*
Kitamura, Satoshi, *illustrator*
Li, Zhao, *author*
Louie, Ai-ling, *author*
Namioka, Lensey, *author*

Say, Allen, *author/illustrator*
Tseng, Jean, *illustrator*
Tseng, Mou-sien, *illustrator*
Uchida, Yoshiko, *author*
Yep, Laurence, *author*
Young, Ed, *author/illustrator*

Latino/Hispanic-American

Ada, Alma Flor, *author*
Allende, Isabel, *author*
Ancona, George, *author/photographer*
Casilla, Robert, *illustrator*
Cortázar, Julio, *author*

Dorfman, Ariel, *author*
Lomas Garza, Carmen, *author/illustrator*
Mohr, Nicholasa, *author*
Schon, Isabel, *author*
Soto, Gary, *author*

Part V

APPENDIX A
Macmillan/McGraw-Hill Selection Review Form

APPENDIX B
Macmillan/McGraw-Hill Editorial Checklist
Recommended Multicultural Opportunities

MACMILLAN/McGRAW-HILL READING
Selection Review Form/Multicultural Consultants

Reviewer's Name: _____   Date: _____

Title of Selection: _____   Grade: _____

Author of Selection: _____

Unit Theme: _____

If the selection is written about your cultural or ethnic group, please comment about the following:

Relevancy: _____

_____

Authenticity: _____

_____

Stereotypes: _____

_____

Historical Accuracy: _____

_____

How would you rate the overall quality of the selection? (Circle one response.)

OUTSTANDING   ABOVE AVERAGE   AVERAGE   BELOW AVERAGE

Use the lines below for further comments. Please suggest information, questions, or discussion prompts that would develop multicultural awareness. In addition, please list any thematically related titles that we could use for the classroom libraries or for the read-alouds.

_____

_____

_____

_____

_____

_____

EDITORIAL CHECKLIST

Selection Title and Author:_____

_____

AUTHOR/SELECTION INFORMATION

ETHNICITY
____ European American

_____

____ African American

_____

____ Asian American

_____

____ Hispanic American

_____

____ Native American

_____

____ Other _____

_____

SEX
____ Male
____ Female

GENRE
____ Play
____ Poetry
____ Historical
____ Contemporary
____ Folktale
____ Myth
____ Biography
____ Autobiography
____ Humor
____ Fantasy
____ Nonfiction/Science
____ Nonfiction/Social Studies
____ Realistic fiction

GEOGRAPHIC LOCATION
____ Northeast U.S.
____ Southeast U.S.
____ Midwest U.S.
____ Southwest U.S.
____ Northwest U.S.
____ Other country

SETTING
____ Urban
____ Suburban
____ Rural
____ Other

CHARACTER INFORMATION

MAIN CHARACTER AGE
____ Young child
____ Teenager
____ 20-30
____ 30-40
____ 40-50
____ 50-60
____ 60 and above
Comments _____

_____

MAIN CHARACTER SOCIAL ROLE
____ Leader
____ Follower
____ Powerful
____ Powerless
____ Victim
____ Victimizer
____ Negative
____ Positive
Comments _____

_____

MAIN CHARACTER ABILITIES
____ Physically disabled
____ Gifted
____ Average
Comments _____

_____

_____

Grade Level:_____ **Editor:** _____
_____

CHARACTER INFORMATION

MAIN CHARACTER ETHNICITY
____ European American
_____
____ African American
_____
____ Asian American
_____
____ Hispanic American
_____
____ Native American
_____
____ Other _____
_____

MAIN CHARACTER SEX
____ Male
____ Female

**MAIN CHARACTER
LANGUAGE USAGE**
____ Dialect
____ Idiomatic
Comments _____
_____
_____
_____

**MAIN CHARACTER
SOCIOECONOMIC SITUATION**
____ Average
____ Poor
____ Rich
Comments _____
_____
_____

CHARACTER INFORMATION

MAIN CHARACTER FAMILY
____ Nuclear
____ Extended
____ Single Parent
____ Foster
____ Adoptive
____ Same Sex
____ Teenaged
____ Stepparent
____ Migrant

OTHER CHARACTERS
(list them and indicate sex and age)
_____
_____
_____
_____
_____
_____

THEMATIC INFORMATION

RELATION TO BANKS THEMES
____ Culture, ethnicity
____ Power
____ Movement
____ Communication
____ Socialization

RECOMMENDED MULTICULTURAL OPPORTUNITIES

BEFORE READING	AFTER READING	OTHER COMMENTS

Part VI

A CELEBRATION OF DIVERSITY:
The Photo Section

A Celebration of Diversity:
THE PHOTO SECTION

The following section of portrait photos is included to supplement the written guideposts for illustrators. The portraits are not intended as specific reference; we expect illustrators to do research as necessary to authenticate their work. The purpose of this section is to serve as a visual guide reflecting the broad and magnificent diversity of people comprising the non-European segment of our nation's community.

We have chosen to focus on the non-European segment of our nation because it is this segment that has historically been omitted from educational materials. By choosing not to include a European-American section, we do not mean to imply that European Americans are not an important part of our pluralistic society.

These photos represent only a smattering of the diversity evident in the thousands of photographs from which we had to choose. Where a single photo is shown to represent, for example, a person of Moroccan heritage, we do not intend to imply that all people of that heritage look alike. We regret that space limitations prohibit including a portrait photo of a person of each gender, from every age group and from every country, culture, region, or nation within the continents represented here.

The portrait photos have been arranged according to the geographic area of ancestral origin. Within the continents of Asia, Africa, North America, South America, and Australia the photos have been arranged by geographic region, and within that grouping according to age. Whenever possible, photos have been identified by the specific area of ancestral origin. Photos which could not be as specifically identified have been arranged more broadly according to age.

Illustrators should use and view the photos in this guide in the broad and diverse manner in which it is intended. Examine these photos for variations in skin tone; facial features; hair color, texture and style. Take note of differences in bone structure, the shape of the face, the eyes, the nose, and the mouth. Look at the color of the eyes, and the fold of the eyelids. Discover the diversity of different age groups and between males and females. Note also that in some photos traditional or ceremonial dress is worn by itself or in combination with typical western clothing. What emerges is a single, yet varied, picture of the diversity around us. Celebrate the richness of our community!

Japan

Japan

Japan

Japan

Japan

Japan

Japan

Japan

Japan

Japan

Japan

Korea

Korea

Korea

Korea

Korea

Korea

China

China

China

China

China

China

China

China

China

China

China

China

Tibet

Tibet

Laos

Cambodia   Cambodia   Vietnam   Vietnam

Vietnam   Thailand   Thailand   Bali, Indonesia

Philippines   Philippines   Philippines   Philippines

Philippines   Philippines   India   India

India

India

India

India

India

India

India

India

India

Pakistan

Pakistan

Pakistan

Sri Lanka

Sri Lanka

Nepal

Uzbekistan

Uzbekistan

Turkmenistan

Afghanistan

Turkey

Turkey

Iran

Iran

Iran

Iran

Iran: Kurd

Iraq

Israel

Israel

Israel

Israel

Israel

Israel

Israel

Palestine

Syria

Jordan

Lebanon

Saudi Arabia

Kuwait

Egypt

Egypt

Morocco

Morocco

African origin

African origin

African origin

African origin

African origin

African origin

African origin

African origin

African origin

African origin

Sierra Leone

African origin

African origin

African origin

African origin

South Africa

Ghana

African origin

African origin

African origin

African origin   African origin   African origin   African origin

Angola   African origin   Mali   African origin

African origin   Ghana   African origin   Swaziland

African origin   African origin   African origin   African origin

Ethiopia

African origin

African origin

African origin

African origin

African origin

African origin

African origin

African origin

African origin

African origin

African origin

Chile

Colombia

Venezuela

Argentina

Peru

Guyana

Brazil

Galapagos Islands

Panama

Panama

Costa Rica

Guatemala

Guatemala

Mexico

Mexico

Mexico

Mexico

Mexico

Mexico

Mexico

Cuba

Cuba

Cuba

Cuba

Puerto Rico

Puerto Rico

Puerto Rico

Barbados

West Indies

Haiti

Antigua

Latin American origin

Latin American origin

Latin American origin

Latin American origin

Latin American origin

Latin American origin

Latin American origin

Latin American origin

Latin American origin

Latin American origin

Latin American origin

Latin American origin

Latin American origin

Latin American origin

Latin American origin

Latin American origin

Latin American origin

Peru: Inca

Mexico: Aztec

Bolivia: Quechua

Ecuador: Inca

SE U.S.: Coushatta

SE U.S.: Seminole

SE U.S.: Cherokee

SE U.S.: Choctaw

SE U.S.: Coushatta

SE U.S.: Mattaponi

SE U.S.: Miccosukee

SE U.S.: Choctaw

NE U.S.: Micmac

NE U.S.: Passamaquody

NE U.S.: Abenaki

S Central U.S.: Osage

S Central U.S.: Cherokee

N Central U.S.: Gros Ventre/Assiniboin

N Central U.S.: Lakota Sioux

N Central U.S.: Wind River Shoshone

N Central U.S.: Lakota Sioux   SW U.S.: Navajo   SW U.S.: Navajo   SW U.S.: Zuni Pueblo

SW U.S.: Cohiti Pueblo   SW U.S.: Navajo   SW U.S.: Navajo   SW U.S.: Navajo

SW U.S.: Tigua   SW U.S.: Pueblo   SW U.S.: Taos Pueblo   SW U.S.: Apache

SW U.S.: Hopi Pueblo   SW U.S.: Hopi Pueblo   SW U.S.: Acoma Pueblo   W Central U.S.: Washo

W Central U.S.: Washo   W Central U.S.: Paiute   NW U.S.: Washington State   NW U.S.: Colville

NW U.S.: Warm Springs   Alaska, U.S.: Inuit   Alaska, U.S.: Inuit   Alaska, U.S.: Inuit

Alaska, U.S.: Inuit   Alaska, U.S.: Inuit   Alaska, U.S.: Inuit   Alaska, U.S.: Inuit

Hawaiian Islands   Hawaiian Islands   Hawaiian Islands   Hawaiian Islands

Hawaiian Islands

Hawaiian Islands

Hawaiian Islands

Papua, New Guinea

Papua, New Guinea

Samoa

Tahiti

Marquesas, French Polynesia

Marquesas, French Polynesia

Fiji

Tonga

Tonga

New Zealand: Maori

New Zealand

Australia: Aborigine

Australia: Aborigine